BLUE

THE COLOR OF NOISE

BLUE

THE COLOR OF NOISE

STEVE AOKI

with DANIEL PAISNER

ST. MARTIN'S PRESS ❦ NEW YORK

First published in the United States by St. Martin's Press, an imprint of
St. Martin's Publishing Group

www.stmartins.com

Designed by Steven Seighman

Library of Congress Cataloging-in-Publication Data

Names: Aoki, Steve, 1977– author. | Paisner, Daniel.
Title: Blue : the color of noise / Steve Aoki with Daniel Paisner.
Description: First edition. | New York : St. Martin's Press, 2019.
Identifiers: LCCN 2019016754 | ISBN 9781250111678 (hardcover) |
    ISBN 9781250111746 (ebook)
Subjects: LCSH: Disc jockeys—United States—Biography. | Sound recording
    executives and producers—United States—Biography. | LCGFT: Autobiographies.
Classification: LCC ML429.A7 A3 2019 | DDC 781.648092 [B]—dc23
LC record available at https://lccn.loc.gov/2019016754

Our books may be purchased in bulk for promotional, educational, or business use.
Please contact your local bookseller or the Macmillan Corporate and Premium Sales
Department at 1-800-221-7945, extension 5442, or by email
at MacmillanSpecialMarkets@macmillan.com.

First Edition: September 2019

10 9 8 7 6 5 4 3 2 1

THIS BOOK IS FOR MY FANS—
TO HELP THEM BETTER UNDERSTAND THE COLOR OF MY LIFE.
WITHOUT THE STEADY, SWEET, GUIDING HAND OF MY MOTHER,
IT WOULD BE A WHOLE OTHER STORY.

CONTENTS

1. Baby When You Say My Name.... 1

DROP

2. You Can Be Who You Were or Who You'll Become.... 14

DROP

3. ... But Terror Takes the Sound Before You Make It.... 19

DROP

4. Where Rocking Horse People Eat Marshmallow Pies.... 36

DROP

5. I'm a Person Just Like You.... 53

DROP

6. Mine to Keep.... 70

DROP

7. Lick the Pavement Clean.... 94

DROP

CONTENTS

8. Wouldn't Be Me Without U. . . .   *113*

DROP

9. We're All a Little Sick. . . .   *123*

DROP

10. Turn Up the Volume. . . .   *146*

DROP

11. Everything That Shine Ain't Always
   Gonna Be Gold. . . .   *169*

DROP

12. Unfuck the World. . . .   *198*

Acknowledgments   *207*

You win only if you aren't afraid to lose.

—ROCKY AOKI

There is no blue without yellow and without orange.

—VINCENT VAN GOGH

BLUE

THE COLOR OF NOISE

1

BABY WHEN YOU SAY MY NAME

Sometimes I think my whole life can be seen through shades of blue. The hope and promise of a clear blue sky. The vast expanse of the deep blue sea. The melancholy that clutches at my heart between the notes of an old blues tune.

The Dodger blue of my cap, when I was invited to throw out the first pitch at Dodger Stadium.

The glistening blue scales that reflect off a fresh piece of kohada when it catches the light in just the right way.

The sweet electric blue of the first-generation BMW i8—the car of my dreams, which to me has always screamed elegance and excellence.

In some parts of the world, blue is the color of mourning. In others, it is an expression of love. In Japan, it represents strength and good fortune.

In our house, when I was growing up, it was the color of how things might have been.

All-time understatement: our house was *way* off the map of most people's experiences. *Way* off the map of what people expect, when they hear pieces of my story. How I came into the world was a little unusual. Wouldn't change a beat, but it wasn't exactly a straight path to finding my way.

I was born in 1977. My parents were together, but only for the next little while. Oh, they loved each other, but not in the same ways. My mother's love for my father was unconditional . . . it was at the core of who she was, very traditional in the Japanese sense. My father's love for my mother was somewhat more ephemeral. If he was in the room with her, living in the same moment, it was a part of him as well. In a lot of ways, he was also traditionally Japanese—proud, devoted, respectful of the institution of family. But he was easily distracted, always looking for something shiny and new, and there were temptations all around. Still, it might have looked like all was right under our roof. On the surface, we were a successful, assimilated Asian family, living our version of the American dream. But underneath that *one big happy* veneer there was the blue of tension, disappointment, anger, sadness. There was love, absolutely, but it was mashed together with so many other emotions it wasn't always clear to me where I fit in the mix.

If I even fit at all.

Here's the deal: my father, Hiroaki Aoki, was a decade or so into a crazy-successful run as the founder of Benihana of Tokyo, one of the most crazy-successful restaurant chains of our time. For as long as I knew him—he died in 2008, when I was just tasting some crazy-success of my own—he was riding high, hard. He was like the Richard Branson of his day—determined to raise hell and to raise his profile in the bargain. He was as big as life—in my eyes, yes, but also to the world, where his reputation preceded him. And now, by extension, it creates a kind of first impression of me, too. Most people I meet, they find out I am "Rocky" Aoki's son, they think they know what my childhood was like. They think they know me and my family. Maybe they do, in a way. Maybe they've been to a Benihana, or maybe they remember reading about my father's adventures. When I came around, he was opening new restaurants all over the world. Out of that, along-side of that, he lived in the half-light of celebrity. He made a bunch of money, spent a bunch of money. His comings and goings made head-lines. He posed for pictures with his famous customers: Muhammad Ali, Mick Jagger, the Beatles. Eventually, some of that fame rubbed off on him. And it didn't just rub off, I don't think. He started living this big, wild life—like the life he'd set out to live could no longer contain him.

My mother, Chizuru Kobayashi, was more of a homebody. If my father's personality was larger than life, hers was small enough to hold in your hand. She is the sweetest person I know—devoted, selfless, cheerful. My father was cut another way. He was the most determined person I ever knew—driven, purposeful, gregarious.

I guess it's true when they say opposites attract. Until they don't.

My parents had been childhood sweethearts back in Tokyo, but my father knew he was meant to live in America. Whatever life there was for him and my mother in Japan, it was not enough—not big enough, not exciting enough . . . not *enough*. For him. For my mother, it was all she knew, all she ever wanted. But my father wanted something more. Something else. He seemed to notice it the moment he set foot on American shores. His first visit to the United States was in 1959, with Japan's national wrestling team. On that tour, he wrestled fourteen times in his weight class and won every match. The only time he lost was when he moved up a weight class and was beaten by a guy who later wrestled for the US Olympic team. That strong showing was enough to earn my father a spot on Japan's 1960 Olympic team as an alternate. He traveled with the team to Rome, but he never got to wrestle. He was on the team, but only in this second-string way—and yet to hear him tell the story later, he was just happy for the thrill of the ride.

He was all about the thrill, my old man. Always. That was his thing. And in some ways, this particular thrill was a kind of placeholder for the thrills yet to come, because he was counting the days until he could return to the United States. He purchased his first car while in Rome—an Alfa Romeo, which he had shipped to New York. It was one of those impulse moves he liked to make. Looking back, it's like his whole life was a string of impulse moves, one after another. He'd get an idea in his head and push it forward, without really thinking it through or talking it over with the other people in his life—like, say, his parents, or his childhood sweetheart, or anyone else who might have been waiting on him back in Japan. He followed the car to New York immediately after the games, telling my mother that he would send for her once he was established.

My father's plan after arriving in New York was to go to college on a wrestling scholarship. He had legit scholarship offers from several schools, but he was holding out for Cornell University. His parents ran a handful of teahouses back in Japan, and his dream was to open a restaurant of his own, and he thought an education at Cornell's prestigious School of Hotel Administration would be his foundation. Trouble was, his English was lousy. He knew enough to get by, but not nearly enough to get by Cornell's admissions officers.

He wound up sharing a crappy apartment on the Upper West Side of Manhattan with a young conductor named Seiji Ozawa, a family friend from back home—yeah, *that* Seiji Ozawa, who would go on to become one of the most famous conductors in the world, a true artist and visionary. In the early 1960s, though, he was just another Japanese kid like my father, chasing his version of the American dream, making his bones as an apprentice conductor with the New York Philharmonic. Years later, whenever Seiji Ozawa's name would come up or we'd see a poster for one of his performances with the Boston Symphony or some other renowned orchestra, my father would tell us his music used to drive him crazy.

I'm guessing Seiji Ozawa, to someone like my father, was soft. Listen to the music he made, most famously as music director of the Boston Symphony Orchestra, and underneath it you can hear the thrill in it, the wild ride, but my father could only hear what was at the surface. He could only hear what he could see.

My father was the deep blue of winter, steeled against the cold, the fighting hue of a wrestler. His roommate was more like the pastel blue of springtime, open to the world and the spirit of renewal.

My father made his nut driving an ice cream truck in Harlem. Imagine that—a Japanese ice cream man, roaming the streets of Harlem. I'm sure it made an odd picture, but this was my father's way. He was most at home when he was out of place—a quality I eventually learned to embrace myself, but only after carrying the weight of feeling like I, too, didn't belong.

The first Benihana of Tokyo restaurant was opened in 1963, on West Fifty-Sixth Street in Manhattan. My grandmother came over from Japan to help my father out. Soon, my mother came over as well, and soon after that they started cranking out kids.

Here it starts to get complicated. Weird, too. My family tree's got a whole lot of branches. There's even a whole other tree—let me walk you through it and you'll see what I mean . . .

My sister Grace came along first, in 1966. Then came my brother Kevin, in 1967. I wasn't born until 1977, but while my mother was in Miami with my brother and sister, my father was shuttling back and forth to New York. In 1975, my brother Kyle was born, to a woman named Pamela—the start of my father's New York family. I guess you'd call him my *half brother*, but we never really thought of it that way, and I only offer the distinction here so readers can keep it all straight. It wasn't about *halves* and *wholes* in our family. It was more about *here* and *there*, who lived under this roof and who lived under that roof.

Kyle's sister Echo was born six months after me. A couple years later, Kyle and Echo were joined by their sister Devon—gifting me, Grace, and Kevin with another half sister.

And then, when I was about sixteen, we learned that my father had another daughter with another woman at around the same time Echo and I entered the picture—our half sister Jennifer, born two months *before me*.

That makes seven children in all: three with my mother, three with Pamela, and one with this other woman who wasn't really in the picture, our birth order all out of sequence. Three of us were born to three different women in a span of about eight months. And for a while our own little subset family didn't know anything about the subset family my father had in New York . . . until his wild ways finally caught up to him and it all came clear.

It was September 14, 1979. I was two years old. My father had taken up speedboat racing four or five years earlier, and in that time he'd become one of the top drivers in the sport. If you go back and look at old newspaper accounts, you'll see he was a real daredevil in those days—that's at least one trait he passed on to me, I guess. He was fearless. There was always some new thrill to be found around every corner . . . sit still and he just might miss it, so he kept moving. The same intensity that drove him to a spot on the Japanese Olympic team and to the top of the restaurant business had quickly pushed him to world-class levels in powerboating. His restaurants sponsored two of the biggest races on the circuit—the Benihana Grand Prix, which had been held at Point Pleasant Beach in New Jersey the previous summer, and the Benihana Grand Prix of Oakland, which was to be held in the chilly waters of San Francisco Bay.

My father was in contention for the national title, and if he won this race he would have been in a good spot to make a run at the world championships in Milan that winter. This was a big, big deal—the thrill of the chase, for a man like my father. But this upcoming race was looking like trouble. My father was concerned about the choppy waters in the tide forecast. He was planning to race his own boat, a banana-yellow catamaran he'd christened *Benihana*—never one to miss a branding opportunity. The cat was one of the only tunnel hulls in the world, built for speed but designed for calmer waters, so he quickly made plans to lease a different boat, a thirty-eight footer that could handle the chop beyond the Golden Gate Bridge. Before deciding which boat he'd use in the actual race, he wanted to take a short run on this new boat to check it out. He had his throttle man with him, a fireman from Fort Lauderdale. The owner of the boat was on board as well, and the plan was for them to take the boat out past the Golden Gate to see what it could do. My father drove, while the fireman controlled the speed, reaching 70, 80 miles an hour, but then about five minutes in something happened. Afterward, nobody on board was able to give an accurate firsthand account, but witnesses said the boat lost its trim and flipped. At that speed, you lose control like that, it's the kiss of death, full on the mouth. The boat pretty much disintegrated, shattered on impact. My father was thrown from his spot behind the wheel and knocked out. The fireman blacked out as well, but he came to soon enough and managed to haul my father and the boat's owner to safety, through shark-infested waters.

It took a while for a rescue crew to reach the wreckage, but my father was eventually taken to a hospital. He was nonresponsive. His pulse was so low, doctors couldn't find it at first. They immediately cut him open and started performing open-heart massage, trying to get the blood flowing. He'd suffered a lacerated liver and a ruptured aorta. His leg was broken in four places. The crash should have killed him, but it didn't . . . not yet. My mother flew out with us kids to be at his side, not knowing that Pamela was flying out to be with him as well, with her two kids—not knowing that Pamela and her two kids even existed!

The crash made news all over the world, and there were dozens of reporters on the scene. It was a real circus. For three days, my father lay in a coma. Nobody knew if he'd survive—and now, as my mother and Pamela were figuring out all these different branches of the family tree, figuring out who they were to each other, who their children were to each other, I guess there were some people in that hospital room wondering how my father would survive the revelations that followed the accident.

I was too little to remember any of this, but I've heard the story so many times it's like an old familiar song. It plays in the back of my head, always, because the moment my father came out of the coma and saw my mother standing there on one side of his hospital bed holding me, with Grace and Kevin standing next to her, and then Pamela standing on the other side, holding Echo, with Kyle standing next to them . . . well, it's like he died all over again.

He turned the mess he'd made into a story—an anecdote he'd spin when he was holding court, telling tales. My father was a great teller of tales. That was his way. He ended up telling the story so many times, it made its way into a newspaper cartoon that came out around that time, showing the great restaurant showman Rocky Aoki in his hospital bed, flanked by a white woman holding a baby on one side and a Japanese woman holding a baby on the other side, with a thought bubble coming from his head: "I'd rather be dead."

Years later, in an interview with a reporter from *New York* magazine, my father told the story with his signature flair, in the broken English that would become a kind of trademark when he spoke to the press. He set the scene by saying, "I'm completely naked, tube in my penis. I see my wife standing over me, on one side. On other side, I see my girlfriend. . . . I say, 'Ohhh . . . shiiit!'"

For the rest of his life, my father would think of his many children as one big happy family, but our reality was a little different. When we were younger, we lived with our mothers under separate roofs, and we kids weren't all together except on special occasions or on vacation with my father. We are close, the siblings, as a group and in our own little pairings. These days, I am especially close to Devon—we move in a lot of the same circles, share a lot of the same spotlight. When I was a kid, I was especially close to Kevin and Grace, even though I was just a tagalong toddler while they were doing their separate things in high school. And for a while Kyle and Echo and I moved around as a group when we were with our father. This was one of the great gifts of our blended family, because I was like an only child at home. I didn't really know my older sister Grace or spend too much time with her when I was super-little, because she was already in high school when I started looking out at the world through my own eyes. Kevin let me hang around, but in truth I only knew him to look up to him. He was always into his own thing. So I loved those times when Kyle and Echo were thrown into the mix with me—and, later on, Devon as well—because I had my little running buddies, all about the same age. Someone to do shit with, make trouble with, share secrets with . . . you know. I'm even tight with Jennifer, in some of these same ways, and she wasn't introduced to any of us until much, much later.

We might have been scattered all over the damn place, connected in all these different ways, sixteen years separating the oldest from the youngest, but the key to me is that we were connected. We were family. Yeah, we each experienced a different childhood, a different reality . . . a different Rocky Aoki. But out of all that, we found our ways to be with each other, on our own, and as the branches of our family tree splintered off in all these different directions, we came to live and work and love and breathe beneath the shade of our own making—the *blue* shade of our own family tree, embedded in our family name. In Japanese, the Aoki name means *blue tree. Ao* can be translated as *blue . . . ki* can be translated as *tree.* And now here we were, thrown together at the same time we were being torn apart by a violent boating accident that nearly killed my father and nearly derailed his family.

One way to look on this great revelation that changed the shape of our blue family tree: my father was an entertainer, a showman, and here the gods of powerboating and Japanese steakhouses and profligate wealth had gifted him with a story. But it wasn't *just* a story. It was a turning-point moment in the life of my family. The skies opened up and the branches of that family tree started reaching for sunlight in all kinds of new ways. And as for me . . . well, I guess you could say this was the moment where I started climbing a branch all my own. I was set down on the path I now travel. Like I said, I don't remember any of it, but in a lot of ways I was born out of those murky blue waters of the San Francisco Bay where my father crashed that boat. My mother had come out to California to be at his side and nurse him back to health, but she ended up divorcing him as soon as he made a full recovery— and out of that our little subset family ended up moving from Miami to Newport Beach, California. After that—in *our* house, at least—my father was in a kind of cameo role: he became like the featured guest star in the movie of my life. He swooped in like some kind of super-hero, bringing tales of his larger-than-life adventures, lighting our world for a short while with the brilliant blue of the horizon at sunrise before disappearing back into a world of his own making.

And there I was in Newport Beach, left to find my own identity in a community where no one looked like me, no one thought like me, and no one seemed to want to have anything to do with me.

I made a promise to myself, soon as I got a sense of who I was and where I was, that wherever I was meant to be I would get there eventually. *Whoever* I was meant to be, I would become that person eventually. Whatever it took. The path that found me in the wake of my father's crash was colored in the blue of doubt and difficulty, but it would take me where I was meant to go.

DROP

There is a famous story about how Benihana got its name, and underneath there is a story about the colors that speak to us in the unlikeliest places:

The streets of Tokyo had been destroyed during the Second World War. Many of the buildings had been reduced to rubble. My grandfather, Yunosuke Aoki, a descendant of a samurai warrior, had been a dancer and choreographer in Tokyo stage productions, but there wasn't a lot of work in the entertainment business when the focus was on rebuilding the country. Wasn't the time to dance, you know. It was time to reach for something new, but in the reaching he grabbed at something familiar. See, he'd also run a jazz club, at a time before the war when the Japanese were hungry to sample American culture, and he'd learned he had a talent for entertaining customers the same way he had always entertained theatergoers.

My grandfather understood that in the aftermath of the war he would have to find a new way to support his family, but he also knew to play to his strengths. He saw a need and he moved to fill it, so when he returned to Tokyo he went immediately to the financial district, where the jazz club had stood. He had an idea to open a teahouse in the same place, somewhere people could gather outside the home and find a shared moment of peace, but the building was a shell, so he looked for another location nearby. While he was looking, he noticed a single red flower, reaching up through the rubble. It was really more of a weed than a flower, but it struck my grandfather as a symbol of hope.

For the rest of his life, he would tell how the red of the flower had popped, like a splash of color against a gray backdrop of ash and ruin.

He saw it as a sign.

He needed a name for his new teahouse, and this lonely red flower was his inspiration. In Japanese, the word benihana is sometimes translated as "red flower." And so he built his shop from the shell of this bombed-out building, and he christened it in this way.

It was just a simple teahouse, serving tea and coffee and small sandwiches and pastries (nothing like the teppanyaki style of cooking my father popularized in the United States), inspired by the appearance of this one brave flower. A red flower—nothing like the blue elements running through this book. But I offer the story here as a reminder that we find our points of inspiration where we can. Each of us looks out at the world in his or her own way . . . and if we're lucky, the world smiles back. We see the colors we choose to see, receive the colors we choose to receive. For my grandfather, this red flower stirred something in him. He could close his eyes and imagine a future for his young family, working long days at the teahouse with my grandmother, Katsu. Bicycling twenty miles each morning before the sun to purchase sugar for his customers, a rare commodity in postwar Japan. Entertaining his customers and offering a place where they could visit with each other and share their stories of struggle and begin to rebuild a sense of community.

In this red flower, he saw hope and renewal. He saw opportunity. He saw a future for his family.

When my father opened his first restaurant in New

York City in 1964, almost twenty years later, he borrowed the name from his father's tea shop back home. His inspiration was not the red of this one resilient flower but the hard work and dedication of his resilient parents, who had somehow found a way to build a life out of no life at all.

Twenty years after that, I would visit one of my father's Benihana restaurants in the United States and be struck by the soft blue tint of the great fish tanks in the entry area. The red of my grandfather's inspiration had faded, and in its place was a whole new American palette, where the aquarium water would shine and shimmy and bathe the room in gentle blue light that spoke to me the same way that red flower surely spoke to my grandfather.

It spoke to me of family.

2

YOU CAN BE WHO YOU WERE OR WHO YOU'LL BECOME

I am my father's son.

He was a showman, after all. A restless spirit. A fearless thrill-seeker. A hard-charger. An entrepreneur.

I am my mother's son as well. A compassionate soul. A gentle spirit. An open mind.

I am the sum of my relationships, my convictions, my hopes for a better planet.

I am a reflection of the lives of my parents. Another chapter in our family's history. An extension of the lives they imagined for themselves.

There's something to this DNA business, yes? We take the genetic material in our makeup, and then we mash it up with the influences that find us along the way, and somewhere in that nature vs. nurture broth we drink deep and discover who it is we are meant to be. Each of us is like a living, breathing remix of all this other *stuff*: the genetic markers we carry, the role models we collect, the styles we grab at and make our own, the cultural norms we embrace or reject . . . they're all a part of us. And they are all stored in one way or another, at one time or another, in the layers of memory. But my memory trips me up. It does. The wiring is slightly *off*. I'll get a story in my head, and it'll stay with me in a certain way for years and years, and then one day I'll re-visit that story with whoever might have been with me at the time, and he or she will tell it from a whole other angle.

Here's what it comes down to, best I can tell:

There is the truth of what I have been told.

There is the truth of what I have lived.

There is the truth of what I remember.

This is the formula, people. Been this way forever. These full-on truths and half-truths and imagined truths are how we get to who we are, where we are, where we're going. Trouble is, what I remember isn't always how things went down, so I'm not always working off the right map. The mind plays tricks—or maybe it's not even paying attention. Most of the time, this is no big thing. It is what it is, you know. It might be that you don't even notice the space between what you think happened and what actually happened. You live so long with a dis-torted version of events that the distorted version is what you remem-ber. But when you go to write a book, you expect to be able to set down the stuff of your life as it was, as it is . . . only as I get started on this I can see there are some pieces missing. Whole chunks. Like that story I told earlier, about how my parents' marriage came apart on the back of that big reveal in my father's hospital room after his accident. That's the way I'd always heard the story, only now that I'm writing about it I've gone back and reread my father's biography and a bunch of old newspaper accounts, and the story takes on a different color. In my head, I was always a newborn—as in, just a couple months old. In my head, my mother had no idea about the other family in my father's life, but of course it was only like that under *our* roof. That was the story we were told, because we experienced the truth of it from my mother's perspective.

A lot of my memories are like that. They go one way. Then I get to talking with someone who knows the deal and they go a different way. There might even be a third or fourth perspective in there, and that takes me off in a whole other direction. And so my thing is to look at where all those stories come together—to find the intersection of what we've been told, what we've lived, what we remember.

I want to get it all down, be a reliable narrator. I want to honor all the people in my life, the stories they keep in *their* heads. Their truth matters, same as mine. The lessons they've drawn from the experiences we've shared . . . they matter, too. And so I'm pumping everyone I know with questions. My siblings. My friends, from back in the day. The people who know me now. I'm having them over to shoot the shit, walk down these lanes of memory with me. I want to know what they know, so I can add it to what I think I know, and then set it all down.

Wasn't until I let the filmmaker Justin Krook follow me around for a documentary on my life and career that I started thinking in this way. I was never big into talking about myself. In my songs, maybe, but not to a journalist or anything. For someone who's as out there and in-your-face as I am with my shows and my lyrics, this might seem like a line, but I always considered myself a private person. That is, until Justin came through. He was hanging around with his crew for a long-ass time, and I started to feel so comfortable around them I almost forgot they were there. He pushed me to talk. About my music, absolutely, but also about what it was like to grow up the way I grew up. About my relationship with my father. My childhood. My family. My *life* . . .

One day, deep into it, I looked up and realized Justin had opened me up, in a way I wasn't expecting. So I turned to him and said, "I'm letting you take a picture of me naked and showing the world."

Justin ended up using that line in the movie *I'll Sleep When I'm Dead*, and it got a lot of play, and that's really how it was. I was stripped-down. Raw. Naked. And after the movie had been out awhile and was making some noise—on the festival circuit, on Netflix—I started to hear back from people how important it was for them to hear me open up in this way. Not just my friends and family, although they were into it. Regular people, who maybe didn't even know my work. Don't know how they came to the movie, must've been plugging in search words like *dysfunctional family* or *demanding father*, but I guess there was something universal in my story. We've all got our own shit to deal with, you know. Demons, skeletons, unresolved issues . . . whatever. It's *how* we deal with them that sets us up for what comes next. It's what we do with what we learn.

And then there were my fans. People all over the world who knew my music but didn't know *me*. They were into it, too. Can't be sure, but I told myself there was a whole new energy to my shows. The energy that was coming back to me from the crowd . . . it was changing up on me. There were more colors to it. Told myself that now that people knew me in a different way, they were responding to my music in a different way. Maybe they were, maybe they weren't . . . but that was the story I started telling myself. And that's when I got to thinking long and hard about seeing if there might be some kind of book in me. A story that was mine to tell, and mine alone. Nothing against Justin Krook, who did a kick-ass job. I'm super-proud of the piece he put out into the world. He got it down and he got it *right*, but that was *his* take on what drives me, and it left me thinking I should take that look myself, see what I can see on my own.

Who knows, maybe the picture that comes back will light a different kind of fire in me, help me to grow my game, connect with my audiences in a brand-new way. Might even get some people to look again at the stuff of their own lives, and spend some time thinking how the ways they were raised might help to guide them on whatever path they're on.

And so . . .

Here is the truth of what I have been told.

Here is the truth of what I have lived.

Here is the truth of what I remember.

DROP

I am the blue of the horizon.

I live and work at the edges of our blue planet.

I stand between where we have been and where we are going.

If all of that sounds like a load of crap . . . well, that's cool. People have said way worse about me over the years. But that's how I've come to see myself, how I've come to set myself. It's become a kind of calling for me to keep ahead of the trends, to dial in to what's happening in the world of music, art, fashion in a way that lets me see what's coming, hear what's coming.

I breathe deep and take it all in, my eyes dead ahead, my ears to the ground, and then I put it back out there so people can find it and taste it and make it their own. So my thing can become their thing. So it can become our *thing.*

I'm like the lookout guy in the crow's nest on the main mast of a ship, keeping constant watch, looking out across the boundless seas on a never-ending quest to spot the hottest new song, new style, new sound . . . This is not me blowing smoke. This is not me inflating what I do or trying to add some cultural significance to my work. No. This is just how I see myself. Really and truly. This is where I stand—at the headwaters of the Next Big Thing, where the sky meets the sea, where the blue of the one kisses the blue of the other and magical things can sometimes happen.

3

...BUT TERROR TAKES THE SOUND BEFORE YOU MAKE IT

Funny the way music finds you when you're a kid. It sneaks up on you. It's in the air, in the mood of the room, all around. And then, when it happens in just the right way, it can get under your skin and hang with you for just about forever.

It's not like you have a whole lot of choice in what you're hearing. Whatever's out there is out there. Whatever's in you is in you. Either you respond to it or you don't. Basically, whatever your older brother or sister is listening to, whatever your parents are listening to, whatever folks in your neighborhood are listening to . . . *that's* what you're listening to—only choice you have, really, is to tune in or tune out.

Me, I tuned in.

Going back as far as I can remember, there was music. Didn't matter that I was four, five, ten years old. Didn't matter if I had a say in what was playing. Didn't matter if it was something I'd never heard before or ever wanted to hear again. It only mattered that it filled the room, or the car. That it filled my soul. Even as a little kid, I *got* that music was who you were—or it was who you wanted to be, and who I wanted to be back then was my brother Kevin. He was my role model, my guidepost, and I saw that oh so clearly when it came to music. He's ten years older than me, so when I started paying attention, he was at that age where he knew what he liked, what his friends liked. I'd be skulking around on the fringes of what they were doing and notice that he and his friends all dressed the same, liked the same things. They rode mopeds together. They wore their hair the same way. Their girlfriends all looked alike. And they all listened to the same music—the Who, The Jam, the Untouchables . . . when I think about those mod bands, I think about my brother and his friends. That was who they were, what they were about.

I didn't understand the music, but I understood that it was a point of connection. It was their common ground, their shared language.

I'd stand on the fringes and take in what I could. Guess you could say I was desperate to see what I could see, hear what I could hear, even if I never had the chance to press Play and listen to my own shit. Never even occurred to me. It was Kevin's shit that mattered just then. When we were kids, it's like he walked on water. I thought he was so cool, so smooth. I thought his friends were so cool. That was the model for me, to be just like them. To have a group of my own friends who all dressed the same and rode mopeds together and dated all those same-seeming girls. I remember going through Kevin's record collection and trying to feel the points of connection he and his friends all felt, the energy, but it was never fully there for me. I got close to it, but I wasn't all the way there. Not yet. It's like I was playing a part, going through the motions . . . *their* motions. The music was only mine in this once-removed way.

And then, a sequined hand just kind of reached up through the noise and grabbed me by the throat.

Now, I don't want to put it out there that Michael Jackson's music was any kind of pathway to my own. Wasn't like that. But his sense of style, his showmanship . . . his *fingerprints* . . . they're all over what I do, and they found me early on, same way my brother's tastes in music found me early on. They informed me. Because, let's face it, when you were a little kid growing up in Newport Beach, California, early 1980s, it was all about Michael.

Understand, I am deeply troubled by the allegations and revelations in *Leaving Neverland,* the HBO documentary that has pushed a lot of people to reconsider Michael Jackson's place in our popular culture—so troubled that for a beat or two I even considered not writing about him at all. But then I realized that Michael's musical trajectory was all tied up in my own, so I'll try to separate the man from the artist. Those songs are out there. Those songs are in me. And the darkness that now attaches to his name cannot extinguish the light that shined in his music . . . the light his music lit in me. Really, I can't overstate the influence Michael Jackson had on our little world. His music was everywhere. The way he dressed, the way he moved, the way he put himself out into the world . . . you could see it, hear it, taste it, around every corner. Style and sound . . . that mix has been at the heart of everything I've ever done as an artist, and here it was, out in force.

Let's be clear, I didn't know what I was seeing, hearing, tasting at the time. And it wasn't necessarily *my* style, *my* sound, but there it was. It's only now, looking back, that I can appreciate the size of Michael's talents. At the time, I knew Michael through his songs on the radio, his videos on television, his billboards on the freeway. I never stopped to think how rare it was for an artist to have such a dominant presence on the music scene, but Michael Jackson was just about everywhere. His music was just about everywhere. His beats, they were like a backdrop to my entire childhood.

Thriller came out in 1982, late. I was five years old—way too young, really, to tap into what was happening. But I got it. Somehow, I got it. I just breathed that shit in. What I remember most from that time was Michael's jacket. You know the one I mean? That slick red turbo-biker jacket with the flared-out shoulders—"the greatest piece of rock 'n' roll memorabilia in history," according to the guy who paid $1.8 million for it at an auction a couple years back. Michael wore it in the "Thriller" video, and it looked like he was from some other planet, dancing across the screen like the absolute shit.

Even at five and six years old, this was what registered. The music. The beat. The look. The whole zombie vibe. Dude had it going on. I watched that video *into the ground*, and then it worked out that I got to see him perform, a couple years later, when I was in the third grade. Michael was still touring off *Thriller*, that record kept sending out hit after hit, and a girl from my class invited me to one of his shows with her parents. Tracie Manzella, she was like my one and only friend. And the thing you need to know here is that I didn't get a whole lot of love from the other kids in elementary school. It just wasn't happening for me, you know. We lived in this plain-vanilla community, and I was the only Asian boy in my grade, and kids have a way of piling on and being really cruel. Sometimes the cruelty takes the shape of indifference—it's like I wasn't even there to a lot of these kids. Sometimes it takes the shape of ridicule—a lot of times I was on the butt-end of some ignorant grade-school teasing. But Tracy didn't care about any of that. Tracy decided she would be my friend—and we still talk, to this day. She's one of the good ones. She used to invite me on these little outings with her family, like to Knott's Berry Farm. And to this Michael Jackson concert. I was seven years old, and I was blown away—at least, as blown away as you can be at seven. The music, I already knew. The moves, I already knew. But the lights and the noise and the pyrotechnics . . . I had no idea how thrilling and how unlike anything else in my experience a live concert could be. The way the audience was completely connected to what was happening on stage, and to each other . . . there was like this deep, fundamental throughline running through the arena. Even at seven, I could feel it. Yeah, there was the music, but on top of that there was everything else, and it was almost overwhelming, just trying to take it all in with my one and only friend.

The thing is, I'd never been to another concert, so I had nothing to compare it to. And it would be a long time before I went to my second concert, so that impression I had of Michael from this one show just grew and grew in my mind. It became larger than life. People toss that expression around all the time, *larger than life*, and a lot of times it's all huff and hype, but here it was really like that for me. I put Michael Jackson on a kind of pedestal. Check that: *he* put himself on a kind of pedestal. He rose to it. He was a presence. He set it up in my mind, what a perfor-mance should be: joyous, exhilarating, a little primal. I didn't know what those words meant when I was seven years old, but I could *feel* these things. For a couple hours that night, I was lifted from my dreary, lonely days and set down on this wild ride. It was so much fucking fun!

So that became my template. Here was this giant of a performer, at the very peak of his powers as an artist, and the takeaway for me was that this was how things should go when you went to a concert.

What the hell did I know, right?

Wasn't like I went back home after that concert and found myself a Michael Jackson clique and started moonwalking all over the neigh-borhood. Michael never became *that* for me and my friends, the way Kevin had this whole mod thing going on with his group, but it was the first time I'd come to a certain type of music on my own, away from my brother's influence. The first time I could see a community coming together, outside of my own house. Out of that one show, I started to see how the kind of music you listened to could shape the way you dressed, the way you looked out at the world, the way you saw yourself in what came back to you on the bounce. It was a way to plug in to your own subculture, and that would eventually happen for me through hardcore, but at the time it was enough that Michael had just held this out there for me, like a promise.

Jump ahead a bunch of years to 2009. Like everyone else I knew, I'd been flattened by the news of Michael's death. It's like all the air left the room the moment I heard. Slap a color on what people were feeling and you can bet it would be blue—the deep blue of melancholy and wistfulness and *what if?*

Michael Jackson's music had made me think of the visual that at-tached to it—the video, the concert, whatever . . . His art was visual, visceral, a full-on assault on the senses. That was one of his great gifts as an artist, the way he tapped into all of that. When I was still coming up as a DJ, still developing my own sound, my own style, Michael's music was a part of that. Almost every night, I'd play at least one Jackson Five tune, one Michael tune. "I Want You Back," "Billie Jean"—those were like my go-to tracks. And when he was gone . . . well, it's like I had to find my way all over again.

Not too long after his death, I got an opportunity to do a Michael Jackson remix. That opportunity found me in my kitchen, of all places. I was fixing myself a cup of tea, doing my thing, going about my day, when the phone rang.

I picked up—said, "Hey."

A woman's voice on the other end said it was Sylvia Rhone, of Motown Records, and I lost my shit. Sylvia Rhone, from Motown Fucking Records. And she wasn't just *from* Motown . . . she was president of the label. I'd never met her, but I knew who she was, of course. Surprised the crap out of me that she knew who *I* was, but there she was, one of the big dogs of the music business, on the other end of my phone. Turned out that part of Sylvia's deal was to oversee the Jackson Five catalogue, which was the jewel of Motown, and in the wake of Michael's death the label was putting together a remix album of Jackson Five tunes. She was reaching out to a bunch of hip-hop and dance producers and DJs—people like Paul Oakenfold, and Pharrell Williams, one of my favorite artists and producers of all time, who'd signed on to do a remix with the Neptunes. Still not sure how it happened, but my name was on her list and she wanted me to participate.

Pinch me, right? Slap me in the face and make sure I'm not dreaming.

The idea, when you put together one of these compilation records, is to feature the most iconic material, which in this case meant "ABC," "The Love You Save," "I'll Be There," "Never Can Say Goodbye" . . . all those great hits. Typically, those tracks go to the top talent involved, and since I saw myself on the low end of the talent roster, I kind of hung back when Sylvia asked me which track I wanted to work on. I didn't want to ask for a song that was maybe a little above my pay grade, know what I mean? That said, I don't remember which one of us hit on the idea of "Dancing Machine," which I'd always thought had this slippery-silky groove to it, a little ahead of its time, but soon as it was out there I was all over it, and soon as we got off the phone I started playing the shit out of that song—just immersing myself in it, you know. Letting it fill me, wash over me.

Took me a while to get to work on it, though. Part of that was me feeling intimidated, being included among all these pioneering artists, working with this legendary material . . . all in service of Michael's memory. That's a heavy deal to throw on the shoulders of a young producer. Got to be honest, I was still pretty green in the studio. Yeah, I was breaking through in the clubs, making some noise, but I was still finding my way, developing my own sound, and it felt to me like there'd be all these eyes on me. All these *ears* on me. People checking me out.

The other part was that it took a long time for me to get the stems from the studio. There was a ton of red tape, moving parts. The Motown lawyers made me sign all these different documents, nondisclosure forms, privacy statements. It was like CIA-level shit, before I could even get my hands on the material. No one outside Motown had ever heard these stems. I had to promise to work on them alone, in my own studio, and to destroy them when the project was complete, and to swear up and down that I wouldn't do anything to jeopardize the privacy or sanctity of the Jackson Five catalogue.

Well, when those suckers finally arrived in my in-box, it was like a birthday present wrapped inside a Christmas gift, all of it tied together with a bow made out of winning lottery tickets. Holy fucking shit! It was such a treasure trove of material, all these little snippets of music history, and I got to mess around with it and put my own signature to it. Really, it was such a blessing to be able to listen to each and every track, and to know that I had been invited to this great party where I would get to create something from this rich, rich material.

For those of you who don't know your way around a studio, a stem is the individual track recording for each element in a song. On one stem, you'll have the bass; on another, some percussion; and then alongside of that you have the lead guitar, the vocals, all the component parts that go into a high-end recording. You can have fifty, a hundred, a hundred fifty stems running through one song, and underneath and alongside there's all this wild sideline shit that never made it to the finished record. You can hear the chatter between the musicians and the engineer. You can hear Michael breathing on his mic, before the take. You can even hear him say, "Alright, alright, let's go . . ." just before the song kicks in. Maybe there'll be an extra bit of percussion or a backing vocal that was never used.

Magic to my ears.

As I listened, I was searching for any hidden elements I could bring to light. Those moments in between, or off to the side, that people might have missed the first time around. So I just kind of went down the rabbit hole, and did my own freaky deep dive, and set off in search of some kind of line I could follow. These stems were just from the final cut, so for all I knew there were hours and hours of additional material in the Motown vaults, outtakes and shit, but this was what I had to work with. One take, broken down into all these precious bits and pieces, and it was on me to find some kind of fresh way to put it all back together again.

The details, they stopped me cold. Michael, breathing. Him and his brothers, just being loose. The back-and-forth chatter. The click of the drumsticks, right before the drums come in. Taken together, it's the song you've heard a thousand times on the radio, but when you carve out each moment it's like you're in the room when it's all going down. It's like Michael has come breathing back to life, and his spirit was right there in my studio.

Hate to get all cliché, but there were shivers running down my spine. Hairs standing up on my arms. All of that.

Chilling. Timeless. Special.

And the thing of it is, you can't change what was. The track is the track. It's not like you can take a broken coffee cup and put all the pieces back together and turn it into a coffee table. But within that certain frame there's a whole lot of play. If it's groovy, you can play with that. If it's funky, you can play with that. You can slow it down, speed it up, turn it on its head. Whatever it was, you can make it more so, or less so, and I sat there listening to all those stems and the time just flew.

Once I had a good sense of the material, I focused on the voice. Whenever I dig in on a new track, my thing is to lay down the main vocal track a cappella. That's job one. You want to make sure the vocal is "dry"—unfiltered, as pure as possible. You can always get back in there and make it "wet," add some reverb to it, some special effect. With Michael Jackson, though, there was no need to doctor his voice. He was just so naturally talented, even as a kid when he set down this "Dancing Machine" vocal, all the way back in 1973. His brothers, too.

After the vocals, I focus on the beat—because, hey, the drums are the spine of the piece, and when you're remixing in the studio there are thousands of beats you can choose from to accent or amplify what's already on the track. Thousands of kicks, thousands of snares . . . you can get lost in all those choices, just hearing what's possible.

From there, you start to build an entirely new track that honors the essence of what the original artist set down, sweetens it, maybe pumps it up a little bit. Everyone at Motown was stoked with what I did with it. When the album dropped—*The Remix Suite*—it got a ton of play, but my cut didn't get a lot of shine, because it was overshadowed by all these top artists and producers, like Akon and Stargate and Wayne Wilkins. I understood that, with where I was in my career, up against where everyone else was in their careers. But the folks at Motown really seemed to dig it, and I got some feedback from the Jackson camp, and end of the day I could slip on my headphones and crank the volume on my "Dancing Machine" remix and feel like I was a part of something.

A part of something Michael Jackson lit in me that night when I went to my first-ever concert.

And with me, what's been lit stays lit.

Jump ahead another few years to 2017. This time the call came to my manager, Matt Colon, who'd been contacted by the folks at Sony and the Jackson estate about another remix opportunity. What was cool about this second go was I was at a completely different place in my career—I'd have the entire Michael Jackson catalogue to choose from, instead of just the Jackson Five material.

I got off the phone with Matt and thought, *Holy shit! I get another chance to do this!*

They sent me a whole bunch of songs to consider, but far as I was concerned there was only one song in the running. I *had* to do "Thriller," right? It was such an essential piece. It got so much play when it first came out, and now, more than thirty years later, it was balls-deep in the culture. It would be like messing with the *Mona Lisa*. But it felt to me like I was destined to reimagine that song, didn't matter how big it was, then or still. There were a couple remixes that came out when "Thriller" was first released, but no producer had gotten his or her hands on the stems from those sessions for the past twenty years, so it would be like making fresh tracks on my snowboard the morning after a big powder dump.

I put it out there that this was the song I wanted to do, the song I *had* to do, and while we were waiting to hear back I got with Matt to talk it over.

He said, "You sure you want to do this?"

I said, "Are you fucking kidding me? If I don't do it, I'll kick myself."

He said, "What about doing something that doesn't come with so much pressure? If it sucks, people will crush you."

This was true, but I didn't care. "Thriller" was like the Matterhorn of American pop music. The pinnacle of the pinnacle. There was no way I could pass on the chance to do a remix of a song that was like the background music to my growing up. To my entire generation. Plus, back of my mind, I knew I could play the hell out of a "Thriller" remix in my sets, knew my fans would really respond to it, so I told myself I was up for the challenge.

Thing is, I really wasn't up to it. Not just yet. What happened was, I kept letting it slide. The track was weighing on me, and weighing on me, and the whole time I was meant to be working on it I was also traveling, on a European tour. I'd grab studio time wherever I could, had my computer with me, my headphones, was constantly tinkering with the thing, playing it over in my mind, but every time I looked up it was like one of those hack scenes in a cheesy movie, the pages of the calendar flipping past until time has just about run out on whatever's going on in the story. I was on a killer schedule—thirty-two shows in twenty-eight days. But that's no excuse. I'm the guy who's always out there saying, "I'll sleep when I'm dead." So that wasn't it. What it was, really, was me feeling a little tentative.

I just don't think I was ready to climb that mountain and slap on my snowboard and have at it.

Course, I wasn't self-aware enough to recognize this. Not yet. I was a little bit in denial, I guess. I was barely getting any sleep, putting it off until I had an idea that felt good, and then I finally charged ahead, convinced myself I was on it, all over it. My take was to make it more like an EDM record—electronic dance music was the world I was in, so that was the vibe I was going for. A heavy, pulsing beat, without a whole lot of the trademark elements of the original. Just some furious sound, to get people going. It would still be a melodic piece, at bottom. There would still be Michael's signature vocal, the spooky essence, but my take was to make it big, big, big. I really wanted to pound out this remix and make it super-big . . . something to make a festival crowd roar.

Progress was slow, but I was getting there. Every week or so, I'd hear through Matt that Sony was calling, wanting to see where I was with the track. Time was really running down—and then, pretty much last-minute, I finished the thing and sent it off. I felt good about it. (Again, what the hell did I know, right?) If you'd have told me I was phoning it in, going through the motions, I would have probably gone off on you. It was an all-consuming thing. Yeah, I had my tour dates, my travel, but this "Thriller" remix was a big, big deal, a top priority, and I'd whipped myself up to that place in my thinking where even though I was pretty damn close to the material, it felt to me like I was really delivering.

A day or two later, we got word back from the Jackson camp that they were into it, and I was looking forward to plowing through the rest of my tour, and to finally being able to play this sucker at my shows once the remix dropped back in the States. Can't tell you what a kick it was to know that Jackie, Jermaine, and Tito and them were digging what I'd done with the piece, but a part of me was holding back. Deep down, I think I must have known there was something missing in the track—and, sure enough, a couple days later I finally heard back from the studio, telling me we were missing a certain "wow factor." That's kind of a catch-all phrase. Doesn't really mean a whole lot, other than that I'd missed the mark.

What was missing, really, was *Michael* . . . that flair he brought to everything he touched. What was also missing was Quincy Jones, who'd produced the hell out of that record. What was missing, too, was . . . well, *me*. I'd put in the sweat and effort, but I was low on heart and soul. Wasn't enough that I'd worked my butt off. Wasn't enough that you could dance to my remix. Wasn't enough that it was big and loud. It needed all those little artistic flourishes, like the Vincent Price narration, the special effects, the sense of mystery and playfulness and innocence that stamped the original. Oh, man, that record was all about the FX! Without all those Michael-type touches, Michael's sense of wonder, my take was just *good enough*—and *good enough*, when you're reimagining the greatest record of all time, just doesn't cut it.

No way.

Bottom line, I needed to spend some more time on it—and the folks at Sony, they were willing to cut me some slack. Whatever deadline I'd just shot past, I'd now have a little more time with the material. Trouble was, I didn't need just a couple days. One of the problems I'd had in that first attempt, I was realizing, was that I'd been a little out of my element. I was working on the fly, away from my usual routines. This was the first week of August, and I wouldn't be able to get back to my own studio until September, but they were willing to wait. I took that to mean either they really, really wanted me to contribute a track—or what I'd sent in sucked so hard I'd left them no choice but to hang back and see if I could deliver.

Soon as I got back home, I did one of those meditative resets. I holed up in my studio and just sat there in silence, for hours and hours. It's like I was lost in prayer, waiting for something to hit me, speak to me.

The idea, really, was to put the world on pause, to shut out everything. The tour had been so fast-paced, always on the go, go, go, it's like I didn't even have time to take a shit. But once I was home, once I was still, back into my own groove, I could take my time. Instead of chasing the material, I could let it come to me. Instead of shoehorning the song into a standard EDM template, I would hang back and see where the thing was meant to take me. So I opened up those stems, one by one, and listened to them all over again. *Really* listened to them. Then I did it again. And again. Got to where I could *feel* Michael Jackson in the room with me. Got to where the hairs were standing up on my arm, the way they were when I first opened those "Dancing Machine" files. After a while, I looked up and realized I'd been in the studio for ten hours, then fifteen, then twenty. I didn't sleep. I didn't eat. For two days, I went at this thing, hard, until I finally emerged with something I *knew* would blow people away.

Thank fucking God the folks at Sony kicked that first version back to me. Really, it was just an overblown, overloaded mess. It wasn't Michael. It wasn't Quincy. It wasn't me. It just *was*, you know. And that wasn't enough. Sometimes you need to stop the train. You need to step back. Because the work has to come from somewhere deep inside you. It can't be rushed or scheduled—otherwise, you're just going through the motions.

The great footnote to this "Thriller" moment was that Michael's father, Joe Jackson, rest in peace, sent word that he wanted to meet with me, maybe listen to the remix in my studio. I laid in some food, some drinks, brought my family out (in part for support, but also because I knew they'd get a kick out of it), and then I waited for Joe to show up with his entourage. I'd already heard that he dug the track, so it's not like I was waiting for a thumbs-up or a thumbs-down, but from everything I knew, Joe Jackson was an intimidating guy. In a lot of ways—from the stuff I'd read about him, heard about him—he reminded me of my own father. When you read the Jackson family lore, you can see a lot of similarities. He was tough on his kids. A no-bullshit type. A real hard-charger. He even looked like my father!

It was a big moment for me, to have this man over to my house, to sit with my sister, my mom, my nieces, and to pay homage in this way to this man's son, the King of Pop. I was nervous AF. A bunch of us squeezed into my studio, we had to bring in extra chairs, and a hush swept over the room as we waited for the track to kick in. And waited. And waited. *I couldn't play the fucking song!* There was some technical issue, and in that tense pocket of downtime I was frantic. I thought, *Fuck! Why can't things go easy?*

But, of course, *easy* was what got me into trouble with my first "Thriller" remix. *Easy* was what people like Joe Jackson and Rocky Aoki never had time for. To guys like that, *easy* was *lazy,* and I think I knew that, in the middle of this tense moment. I knew that whatever approval I was seeking from this archetypal father figure, it would not come easy.

I had to restart my whole system, and then I finally played the song, and Joe seemed to really vibe on it. Then I played it again, a little louder. And then again after that, louder still.

Each time out, the energy was different.

Each time out, there was more urgency, more *Michael,* and somewhere in there, third or fourth time through, I could close my eyes and picture myself back at that first concert, with my one and only friend, Tracy Manzella, realizing for the first time the neon-blue power of music, the ways it can lift you, shape you, help you to feel a part of something bigger than yourself.

DROP

I am flying. Really.

I no longer know where I am going, where I have been.

I am in the middle of a long-ass bus tour. Thirty-three shows in thirty-six days. It's a fucking marathon, and when the bus can't get me where I need to be, I hop on a plane and jet back and forth. Put a pin on the map, wherever we are, fly back to the bus, and continue on our way.

There's a copy of today's New York Times *folded in on itself and stuffed into the seat-back cushion in front of me. Or maybe it's yesterday's paper—I'm no longer sure of the date, either. Whatever. Can't remember the last time I cracked an actual newspaper. It's old-school. These broadsheets, with the leaky newsprint . . . it's the way my father used to read the paper. Somebody told me they have classes on how to read the* Times, *how to spread out the paper and fold it lengthwise into long accordion sections, and then again from the top down—the only way to read the damn thing on a subway. Or a tour bus.*

I pull out the paper, start to read. I am drawn to the obituaries—to one in particular, for an artist named Gary Burden, who designed all these iconic album covers. They give him a half page, so you know the guy was the real deal. I don't recognize the name, but I see that I know his work. I see that his work mattered. There are thumbnail images of familiar album art, covers I've seen over and over to where I can even attach the

accompanying songs to what I'm seeing: the Doors . . .
Crosby, Stills & Nash . . . Neil Young.

Here is a shot of the cover of Joni Mitchell's Blue—*one of Gary Burden's covers, apparently.*

Here is a quote pulled from an interview with Gary Burden on NPR's World Cafe: *"How to visualize the music. That's been my obsession."*

Mine, too. Always, I think in terms of what I'm seeing as I play my music, what my fans are seeing. Back when music videos were relevant, prevalent, you could maybe manipulate the visual, help the listener out, get him or her to imagine what you were imagining. But now, it's back to what the music tells you. It's whatever mood you're able to create, whatever colors come along with that.

I am floored by the connection. The serendipity of it. I mean, what are the odds? This book you now hold in your hands, open to this very page, it is on my mind as I ride the bus, as I bounce from city to city. I write as I move. I write as I breathe. I reach for the shades that color my music and try to put them into words. And here is this obituary of this giant album artist, someone who put his fingerprints all over these classic records, helped us to "see" these classic artists as they didn't know they wanted to be seen. As they were meant to be seen.

I set the paper down and think what it means, me coming across this obituary, at just this time in my life. It's not about me, I know. Somebody died. He had a wife. He left a mark. So, yeah, it's about him. Gary Burden. But running into him like this, learning the story of his life and career, reading about how he would try to visualize the music with his designs, seeing what we might see before we could see it for ourselves . . . it's almost cosmic. That Joni Mitchell album cover, staring back at me. The artist, half in shadow, lost in song, lit by shades of blue. It's like this folded-up newspaper was left here for me. It's just too, too much.

Blue.

I find the album online, start to listen. Some of the songs I know. Some I don't. The title song, "Blue"—it's possible I'm hearing it for the first time, because it doesn't feel familiar. It's not a part of me. Yet.

"Songs are like tattoos," Joni Mitchell sings. Yeah, they are. We wear them on our hearts. They become a part of us. We reflect what we hear and put it back out into the world, so everyone else can hear what we're hearing.

4

WHERE ROCKING HORSE PEOPLE EAT MARSHMALLOW PIES

S o. Over the course of our lifetimes, there are moments that define us or shape us or move us in some new, meaningful way.
    There are moments that catch us leaning one way and then
going another.

And the thing of it is, these moments find us under the same open
sky. We all live beneath the same blue canopy of hope and possibility,
in a world where just about anything can happen—and it sometimes
happens that the good that finds you and the evil that alights in you
wind up meeting in the same damn place at the same damn time.

Crossroads, man. That's what I want to spend some time on here:
roads taken and not taken. Decisions made and unmade. Points of
departure that set us off in a whole new direction we might never have
thought of taking. We've all been in one of those spots. We go through
the motions and do our thing and then we look up and realize, *Hey,
that was where it started for me.* Or, *That was where it ended.*

Whatever.

In a lot of ways, where it started for me, this path I'm on now, and
where it ended for me, that path where I was just so fucking desperate
to fit myself in and feel like I belonged, crossed on one epic night in

high school. Ninth grade. I was thirteen years old—one of those late-birthday kids. Everyone else was fourteen. My afternoons consisted of hanging out with my friend Brian and playing *Street Fighter* at a pizza joint called Moe's. We'd pinch a couple quarters from the money our moms gave us for lunch at school to have enough left for a slice and some games.

After school . . . weekends . . . we'd be dropping quarters down at Moe's—because, hey, what the hell else were we gonna do?

One afternoon, this other kid came in and started talking to us. Let's call him Mike—don't want to mess him up by calling him out. Mike was like the school fuckup. One grade ahead of me, two years older than me. I looked up to him, thought he was just about the coolest guy on the planet. He was always missing class, always in and out of trouble. Lived outside the lines, you know. That was very appealing to me—still is, in a lot of ways. Not because I was looking to cut corners and cause trouble, but because I was out to shake things up. Because I wasn't content to sit back and do what everyone else was doing, what was expected.

Because there were no rules—and one thing I'd learned from my father was that life was one giant ride.

Mike sat down next to us, and Brian and I flashed each other these looks—like, *Why is this guy even talking to us?* We were lowly freshmen, right? But Mike had some acid he wanted to sell and there was no one else around to sell it to. At the time, I just thought we were hanging out—but to Mike, we were a business opportunity. He spent about a half hour telling us about this "funny paper" he had that would just make us laugh and laugh. He didn't call it acid. He didn't say it was illegal or potentially hazardous to our mental health or adolescent sense of self-esteem or anything like that. Just said it would be the most ridiculous fun.

Said it would be way more interesting than hanging out at Moe's, eating pizza and playing video games—and, got to say, Mike was damn fucking right.

He handed over a little square piece of paper with a cartoon-y stamp of a bomb on it, to show us what he was talking about. It looked like a page torn from a comic book. Oh, man . . . I was such an idiot. Talk about colors—I was green all over! I suppose on some level, deep down, I could see this moment for what it was, but on the main level, where I lived and breathed, it was completely innocent. What it came down to, really, was that I'd placed Mike on this pedestal of cool and wanted him to think I was cool, too. And whatever it was Mike was selling us, Brian said he'd tried it once before and it was crazy-ridiculous, and we should so totally go for it, so after a whole lot of back-and-forth we decided we'd split one and do it together.

Mike wanted five bucks for this little piece of paper—don't know that it was worth five bucks, but I appreciated that he'd invested a ton of time with us, trying to coax us into buying, so maybe he factored in his time as well. I literally had four quarters with me, and Brian didn't have any money, so we hopped on our bikes and rode to our houses, told Mike we'd double back. My house was about three miles away, so I had all that time to think about what I was doing, but it never occurred to me that I was doing anything wrong, or bad, or dangerous. Yeah, I'd heard about acid, but *this* wasn't *that*—this was just a funny piece of paper that would make me laugh.

Anyway, that's the way I spun it in my head.

At home, I found another $1.50, digging through drawers and pockets, to cover my share, then I rode back to meet Brian, who'd gone home to find his half of the money, and we met back up with Mike and did the deal.

(I think we paid him in quarters—makes me laugh my ass off to think about that now.)

Keep in mind, I'd never done anything like this before in my little-kid life. I'd never smoked weed, never even had a beer. I hadn't done shit. Already, I was drawn to the spirit of straight-edge hardcore, a subculture of the punk movement where everyone swore off drugs and alcohol and tobacco. Already, I saw something in the few straight-edge kids I knew in school that I wanted to emulate, something that spoke to me. And the music . . . man, I loved the raw, stripped-down energy of the hardcore bands my friends were listening to. I'd started to think I could fit myself into this crowd, same way my brother had his mod friends when he was in high school. This was what was click-ing, just then, what I was feeling, so this deal I had going with my friend Brian was *way* outside the lines for me. Still, a part of me must have known I was taking some kind of turn, because I said to Brian that I wanted to hold on to the paper Mike had handed over to us, which was wrapped in tinfoil. Why? Can't really say, except that Brian had already tried it, and I guess I wanted this sense of ownership over this thing. Or maybe I just wanted to live with the idea for a while, try it on, get my head around it, see what it felt like to move around like a kid about to do whatever it was we were about to do.

A couple days went by, and I still had that tinfoil in my pocket. All day long, I'd touch my hand to my pocket and feel its shape, feel its power. Just knowing it was there made me bad-ass. I looked around at all the other kids who didn't have a hit of acid in their pockets, and knew I had something on them, was headed somewhere new, differ-ent. And now here it was, a Friday night, and I was with a bunch of people at our high school basketball game. I was on the fringes of this other group of kids, my snowboarding buddies, and most of them were older than me. Just as innocent, probably, but a couple years older. They were into hardcore, same as me, but I couldn't say if straight-edge was part of their vocabulary. I mean, they were straight— meaning most of them didn't drink or do drugs—but if I had to guess, with this group that probably had more to do with a lack of opportu-nity to mix it up and party than it did with any hard-won principles.

Brian wasn't with us, but the loose plan was that we'd meet up later and do our funny business. I was sitting in the bleachers, half-watching the game, half-thinking I was a total fucking loser to be sitting in the bleachers on a Friday night with my total fucking loser friends, watch-ing a basketball game. Nobody else in the school paid any attention to us—and, most of the time, we didn't give a shit about them. Don't know why we were even there, in the bleachers, playing at high school, but it was something to do, I guess. Someplace to be. And somewhere in there I touched my hand to my pocket and felt the outline of that little fold of tinfoil. I started thinking about this kid Mike, about what a bad-ass he was, about what a bad-ass I wanted to be. And then I started thinking, Fuck it. Fuck Brian. I'll just go ahead and do this. Right now.

I ducked out to go to the bathroom, and as I was standing in front of the urinal, peeing, I reached into my pocket and opened up the tinfoil, saw the little paper with the bomb on it. The idea was we were going to break it in half, and Mike had said that would be enough for both of us, but that wasn't part of the equation I was running in my head in this moment. No, this moment was all about me being a complete bad-ass. Breaking the rules. Going for it . . . *hard*. I'd spent all that time worrying over that stupid piece of tinfoil, and here I just tore it open and swallowed the piece of paper like it was a piece of candy—*boom!*

I had no idea what would happen next, how things would go. I didn't know shit about shit. I went back to the bleachers and sat down next to this friend of mine, Rob, and told him what I'd done. I had to tell somebody, right? Rob was my closest friend in that group, so he got the nod. I don't think I called it acid, though. I was still using the language Mike had used with us. Funny paper. But Rob knew. The other kids we were with, they knew.

One of them said, "What the fuck, man? How did you get your hands on some acid?"

To them, I was just this scrawny little Asian kid. I was just tagging along to this basketball game, same way I seemed to tag along when we went riding, and here I just dropped this bomb on them, that I'd ducked out to the bathroom and taken a hit of acid.

They thought I was fucking with them—said things like, "You're full of shit, man."

I stuck to my story, kept insisting I'd just swallowed this piece of paper with a cartoony bomb on it, and eventually I convinced them I was dead serious. Yeah, I might have been full of shit about some stuff, but I was way too specific to be full of shit about . . . *this*.

A couple of them started freaking out, said I was gonna die, said I'd taken too much, and I started to panic, went outside and tried to make myself throw up behind the bushes near the gym door, but of course by that point whatever I'd taken was already absorbed into my system, and even if I did manage to hurl that piece of paper it wouldn't have made a fucking difference.

I went back to the snowboarders, and one of them decided he would be my designated acid buddy. Let's call him Alex. He was a senior, the adult of the group—the exception to the straight-up loser vibe the rest of us were putting out. He had a truck, drove us around. He said, "Yo, I've done acid a bunch of times. Hang with me, Steve. I'll take care of you."

And so it was decided. I took off with Alex and we went for a drive. We weren't headed anywhere, just driving. I remember looking out at the most mundane things and just cracking up. I'd see two red cars, and I'd say something stupid like, "Those cars are identical." Then I'd laugh and laugh. In my mind, the way it was working in that moment, the two cars were one and the same. Everything was illuminated, more real than I'd ever seen or experienced. Everything made sense, and nothing made sense.

Alex was a good guy, but he was also fucking with me a little. He'd see me fixed on something—a red light, say—and he'd say, "You sure that's real, Steve? You sure you're not just imagining it?"

I don't think I ever laughed so hard in my life, before or since. My stomach was hurting from laughing so hard. I was crying-laughing. It was the most fun I'd ever had—supersized, warp-speed fun. Felt to me like it would never end.

And then, just like that, Alex said he had to go home. It was maybe two o'clock in the morning, and I wasn't done laughing. But just hearing from Alex that he was leaving put me on edge. I was spooked, a little bit, at the thought of being alone. It hit me in this all-of-a-sudden way. Alex had been like my spirit guide through all this, had kept me anchored in this place of lightheartedness.

Alex could see my mood downshift, so he tried to reassure me—said, "I'll take you to Rob's house. He'll take good care of you."

It's telling, looking back, that it wasn't even an option for Alex to drop me off at my own house, but it was just me and my mom and my grandfather, and they would have been asleep, and I was in no shape to be left alone.

When we got to Rob's place, his whole family was up. That strikes me now as weird, that they were all up at two o'clock in the morning, but there they were. Maybe Alex had somehow called ahead. Maybe I was just paranoid. Whatever it was, one by one, they all came over to check me out. His parents had been given to understand that somebody had fed me some drugs, and I remember getting this intensely negative vibe. Underneath all that patience and concern, I went from light to dark. It was like being in the Upside Down in *Stranger Things*, a whole other dimension. Nothing seemed to make any sense, all the fun and lightheartedness just fell away. There was one moment in there, Rob and I were watching one of those old televisions with a rabbit-ear antenna, and the picture just started to scroll, like there was a problem with the horizontal hold. We were watching an old *Tonight Show* rerun, and Johnny Carson's face kept popping up and down, and I looked over at Rob, lying on the bed next to me, and said, "You seeing this shit?"

He'd been asleep, tried to adjust himself awake—said, "What shit, man?"

Whatever shit it was, I was getting into it, deeper and deeper.

Another flash memory from that night: I had this vivid image of being inside a Gwar video. Gwar was this metal band we used to listen to, and their thing was to dress as these crazy, evil-looking monsters. They were, like, over-the-top grotesque, and when you weren't tripping your ass off it was cool as hell, but when you were fucked up and unhinged and feeling like the world was spinning away from you it was completely terrifying. These dudes were chasing me, throwing battle-axes and fireballs at me, and I remember feeling naked and vulnerable and scared out of my fucking mind. And it was all so *right there*. My eyes were closed, but it's like the scene was playing out on an IMAX screen on the inside of my eyeballs.

A part of me knew it was a movie of the mind, a fantasy, but another part believed it was real and that I was doomed.

Rob must have drifted off to sleep by this point, because I was on my own in this. There was no one around to tell me I wasn't stuck in this world where these monsters and villains were trying to chase me, trying to kill me. No one to talk me down from the shit I was in.

I caught myself thinking of the nuns back in Catholic school. Don't know what it was that had me making this leap, but in my head I went all the way from Rob's bedroom to one of those classrooms at Our Lady Queen of Angels, where the nuns used to make us stand at the chalkboard and draw our vision of hell. How fucked up was that? But that was just a typical day at school for us, and here I was, on the dark side of this lonely acid trip, imagining myself back in the front of the classroom, drawing a burning lake of fire—the nun saying, "If you don't believe in Jesus Christ, you'll burn in this pit of fire forever and ever."

The decision to send me to Catholic school was my mother's, long as I'm on it, and it had nothing to do with her religious views at the time . . . or mine. Wasn't like that in our house. At first, sending me to Catholic school was just a way to keep me focused, in line. I had trouble making friends. I was super self-conscious as a little kid, felt like I stood out, and not in a good way. So my mom sent me to Copre Christian, because she thought in a private-school setting I'd get a little more attention, maybe there'd be a couple extra sets of eyes on us kids in the playground, whatever. But I still had a tough time, even in second and third grade. I used to act out, I guess, and the teachers back then would spank you with a huge paddle if you were any kind of discipline problem. It was fucked up, so after a while my mom pulled me out and sent me back to the public elementary school, where at least they didn't paddle your ass. Only that didn't work out too well, either. I started getting into fights, mostly over stupid racist shit—mostly with *me* on the receiving end of the stupid racist shit (although I'll confess, after a few too many taunts and beat-downs I learned to give as good as I got). I struggled in the classroom, too, so for middle school my mom decided to change things up again, this time sending me to

Our Lady Queen of Angels, where the fuckedupedness continued, this time with those nuns using damnation and hellfire as motivational teaching tools.

Eternity—that's what the nuns were selling us. It's like they were scaring us into faith. That was their deal. And they made sure we understood what eternity meant, inducting us into this kind of cult of Christianity that was built entirely on fear. Fear of God. Fear of stepping off some righteous path. Fear of the unknown. Fear of *not believing*. I'd taken all of that in as a kid and set it aside, first time around at Copre Christian, and now it all came rushing back to me following this rookie acid trip. I was filled with this slow drip of dread and anxiety. And from that point on it felt to me like I passed the whole rest of that night staring at the ceiling in Rob's room. Every second felt like an hour. Every hour felt like a day. The time just dragged. And with each passing moment it felt to me like I was being sucked from the bed and lifted to the popcorn tiles of Rob's bedroom ceiling. The little bumps and dimples on those tiles seemed to take on new shapes the longer I stared at them—they were getting bigger and bigger, and trying to swallow me up and leave me marooned on this giant moonscape of popcorn tile.

I was sure this was how things would be for the rest of my life. There'd be no end to it. I'd be swallowed up by these puffs of plaster, or attacked by battle-axes and fireballs, or tossed into some burning lake of fire. Everything I was feeling, everything I was seeing, everything I was imagining . . . it was all rooted in fear.

And there was no escaping any of it. Only way out was to just give myself over to it. Or kill myself. I wasn't suicidal or anything, but in the twisted logic that comes with a hit of acid I caught myself thinking death was the only way to quiet the raging noise and nonsense inside my head.

It all seems so clear to me now, that this was just the acid messing with my head, but while I was stuck on the dark, mindfucking edges of whatever trip I was on, there was no such thing as clarity. There was only confusion. Panic. Unimaginable doom and gloom. And even if a fleeting, reality-based thought snuck its way in, reminding me that the funny paper I'd swallowed was fucking with me, I'd start to think I'd come down from this trip and be so completely screwed up they'd have to put me in a mental institution. My wiring would be all off, here on in, and I'd be on the edges of this mindfuck forever.

I look again at this weird-ass night and how it came about and I'm struck by the tug-and-pull between good and evil, light and dark, innocent and jaded. In the story of my life, the story I keep telling myself about how I came to hold the values that now define me, how the person I've become was allowed to take shape, everything points to this one moment. Something to think about: the whole thing came about on the back of this school fuckup, Mike, trying to sell us a hit of acid, something that was actually *bad* for us, by telling us it was *good*, and *harmless*, and *fun*. And then it ended with me dead awake, thinking of the nuns back in Catholic school, selling us something that was actually *good* for us by trying to scare us into believing we would dwell in an everlasting hellscape if we didn't buy in.

Remember those cartoons we used to watch as kids, where the character had a devil on one shoulder and an angel on the other shoulder and he was stuck trying to figure out some serious shit? That was me—I was stuck, man. Torn. Ripped apart, in fact. Wasn't anyone I could tell what was running through my head. I couldn't talk to my mother—no way she'd understand the trip I was on. My father wasn't really a daily presence in my life, and the couple times a year we were together as a family, there wasn't really room in our routines for a full-on discussion of faith and fear and fucking up. (Plus, he was a Buddhist by tradition—although, best I could tell, he didn't buy in to *any* of this religion stuff.) I couldn't tell my brother or sister—they were out of the house, off living lives of their own. I couldn't tell my other siblings. My friends weren't the kind of friends I could talk to about this shit, and even if I could, they'd only hear the parts that were fun and wild and out of control.

By the time the sun came up and my head wasn't tingling and the bumps on the popcorn ceiling tiles weren't trying to suffocate me, things weren't any clearer. Rob went to the kitchen and brought me a glass of orange juice, said it would be good for me—only I couldn't seem to get the straw to work. I'd suck and suck and the juice wouldn't go down, wouldn't reach my lips. Rob watched me struggle and thought it was the funniest fucking thing, but I got it in my head that in order for me to take in this nourishment, in order for me to restore myself and somehow be made right and whole, I'd have to accept Jesus Christ as my Lord and Savior. That's where I went with my thinking— the consequence of this one transaction. That fear and dread that had been drummed into my head so mercilessly, so joylessly by the nuns at Our Lady Queen of Angels just reached up and grabbed me by the throat, told me I had better fall into line or I'd be locked up in some mental institution, or staring into some desperate abyss of loneliness or fuckedupedness or depression.

Those crossroads I talked about earlier? Here I was, at this giant fork in the road, and the path I chose was faith and purity. In *that* moment, struggling like an idiot to take in a couple sips of orange juice, I swore off drugs. I swore off alcohol. This was the pivot point into straight-edge for me—I remember it like it happened yesterday. Wasn't like I was giving up all that much, because I'd never done any of that stuff before this one wild night. But I'd been scared straight, decided I'd become a hardcore Christian. I vowed to live a more faith-based life. A life of meaning and purpose. It was who I was, I told myself. Curiously, it was a decision that came from a place of fear. I'd been exposed to all that stuff when I was a kid in Catholic school, had always stiff-armed the rituals of organized religion, but now that I'd stared eternal hellfire in the face I'd come crawling back to it.

And so, out of that one night, the fog of Mike's funny paper finally lifted, I started going to church, started listening to straight-edge hardcore music. Yeah, my music was angry, but my heart was pure. And even though I might have been drawn to God and religion for the wrong reasons—or at least not enough of the *right* reasons—I found that my little-kid life now had a purpose. I was on a path. Oh, I'd still hang out at Moe's and suck back those slices and drop quarters into the *Street Fighter* machine, but more and more I started losing myself in the intensity and fury of the music I was listening to, the bands I was going to see.

Somewhere in there, I went to a couple Christian hardcore shows— just, you know, to check them out. And at that time in my life, I tried to get behind the spirit-filled lyrics. I tried to let the words fill me, run through me. I wanted to find myself between the lines of the songs from bands with names like Outspoken and Unashamed and Unbroken. I wanted to shout about Christ and righteousness and clean living. I was all about it. Got to where I was making my mother these Christian-themed pottery pieces in my art class at school—wooden cutout fish, coffee mugs with a cross on the side.

Going to those straight-edge hardcore shows . . . that became my scene, my thing. My lifeline. And it's only now, revisiting my evolution, that I can see the poetry in it, you know. Only now that I can understand the journey I was on. The way the acid spoke to me. The way these songs spoke to me. The way the shards of my Catholic school education spoke to me. Even the labels that attached to the names of my favorite bands spoke to me, told me I wasn't alone.

Outspoken.

Unashamed.

Unbroken.

In the end, the big takeaway for me was coming to the realization that hardcore music could be a refuge for outcasts and iconoclasts who don't feel like they belong anywhere else. Every song was about finding your voice, finding your community, finding your way. The lyrics spoke to this sense of standing up for who you are, who you're meant to be. And it wasn't just the lyrics; you'd go to these shows, and the guy on the mic would spend more time talking about the song and telling you what it was about than he would actually singing it. That was the style, and I soaked up all of *that*, too.

I'm in a different place now—although I still live a clean life. I stepped off that path for a while, but now I'm back on it, back at it. For a whole mess of new reasons, and a few holdover reasons from when I was a kid, I will always be hardcore, at my core. But I don't grab at the Christian dogma the way I did as a confused thirteen-year-old, the way I did through most of high school. I don't preach or follow the rule book. I think of myself more as a Student of Life than a Child of God. I might go to church from time to time, just to listen to what they have to say, but then I'll go to some other church and listen to what *they* have to say.

To me, faith is not about belief or disbelief. It's about being open or closed. And me, I'm open wide.

I am the blue of the open sky, eager to take in whatever the world has to teach me.

Whatever *you* have to teach me.

The great footnote to this story is that things have kind of flipped between me and my mother. When I was in high school, it was me moving the conversation along in this way, toward God and religion. For my mother, going to church was more about being a part of a community than it was about belief. She went to church because that was just what you did. It wasn't any kind of big deal—only now it's huge. My mother has deepened in her faith, while I have softened in mine, but I can't let her know I have any doubts, or that I'm not exactly where she is on this, because it'll freak her out to think I don't believe. The way she's got things figured, the people you love have got to believe in Jesus Christ if you expect to see them in the great hereafter, and I don't have it in me to tell her any different.

Truth is, she got this way from me. I was the one, all the way back in high school when I was shouting the word of Jesus Christ, trying to get my grandfather to believe. He'd come to live with us for a stretch, and with my father out of the daily picture it was my grandfather in that *father figure* role. He was an interesting character, my beloved *ojii-chan*. Years later, my mother told me stories about how he was caught in the swirl of the yakuza, the vast network of Japanese organized crime syndicates, how she traveled to find him in the mountains of Sapporo, on the island of Hokkaido, in the northern part of Japan. She went to rescue him, to draw him back into the circle of family, to bring him home, and he eventually came to live with us in Newport Beach. For most of my growing up, it was just the three of us in the house—Mom, Ojiichan, and me. I looked up to my grandfather, tried to carry myself like him, wanted to keep him in my life as long as possible, so when he got older and I went all Christian hardcore I'd start selling him—same way the nuns used to sell me. I'd say, "Please believe in Jesus Christ, because I want to see you in heaven."

Every night, as his health turned and he started to lose his strength, I'd tell my grandfather how much me and my mother needed him up there in heaven, watching over us, waiting for us. I'd tell him how it was no big deal, just to say he believed, as a kind of insurance policy. I'd say, "If you don't believe, you'll go to hell."

Insurance.

That was like a synonym in our house for *belief.* My thing was, if you couldn't buy in wholeheartedly, if you couldn't give yourself over to a life in service of Christ, you could at least go through the motions and ask to be counted—you know, as a kind of hedge. My grandfather died at the age of eighty-eight. And best I could tell, best my mother could tell, he was on God's insurance plan. He'd said as much, anyway, and I was only too happy to believe him.

Jump ahead to the here and now, and it's my mother selling the same shit back to me, using the same language I used on my grandfather. Her father. She'll call me up almost every day and say, "Don't forget the insurance plan." Or she'll text. I can show you this endless thread in my phone: "Don't forget insurance."

It's super-sweet—but she's dead serious, firm in her beliefs, convinced that I must be firm in mine if we expect to see each other in the blue of the great beyond. So I play along—only I'm not playing along, really. I *do* believe, in my own way. I wouldn't call myself an atheist, and I have difficulty calling myself a Christian, but I'm open to whatever it is that's out there. I'm accepting. I'm willing to ride whatever wave the folks around me are on and see where it takes me, and along the way I'll take time to treat people decently, to live a good and noble life, to make the world a better place in whatever ways I can, big and small.

The more I learn, the less I know . . . that's pretty much what it comes down to, for me.

Insurance? Religion is not about that for me, not anymore. Faith is not about that. I don't live my life in fear of the unknown—got all the insurance I need here on this earth. But what I learned from this one wild acid trip that set me off in search of some deeper meaning and feeling of connectedness is that you just never know how things are gonna go.

DROP

A friend recommends a novel called The Leavers, by a Chinese-American writer named Lisa Ko. It was nominated for a National Book Award. I see on the description that it's about the child of a Chinese immigrant being raised in a white neighborhood by his adoptive white parents. I get why my friend says I should read it—but then I get this shit all the time. The people who know my story, where I come from, know the ways I feel connected to other fish out of water.

They know how it colored me to grow up as one of the only Asian kids in a lily-white, same-seeming neighborhood like Newport Beach, California.

They know I move about the planet like I'm on the outside looking in, always trying to make a place for myself.

No, this character's story is not my story. This character's experience is not my experience. But I get a copy of the book and start to read. In disconnect there is connection, I guess.

Right away, I get that this Lisa Ko is a gifted writer. I am struck by the sweet strength of her voice, by the weight of isolation in her story. It's good stuff. I am also struck by this one passage, early on, that speaks to the power of music. See, the main character plays the guitar, is big into music, and we live inside his head as he thinks about what his music has meant to him on his journey to belonging.

Check it out:

"Never had there been a time when sound, color, and feeling hadn't been intertwined, when a dirty, rolling bass line hadn't induced violets that suffused him with thick contentment, when the shades of certain chords sliding up to one another hadn't produced dusty pastels that made him feel like he was cupping a tiny, golden bird."

That passage just blows me away. Still. I go back to it from time to time, attach it to the collective din that fills my senses, fills my soul. It's in my head, every time I push my fans at my shows to make some fucking noise. It is who I am, what the music means, where it can take me. Where it can take us. Together.

Fuck, yeah.

5

I'M A PERSON JUST LIKE YOU

Music was everything. One day I looked up and it was in the air, on my clothes, coursing through me.

Couldn't shake that shit for tryin'.

Here's the deal: music filled the spaces where the rest of my life might have been. It lifted me from a place of disconnectedness and loneliness and confusion and opened me up to a sea of possibility—a deep blue sea, long as I'm thinking in colors.

Yeah, yeah, yeah, I get that the ocean isn't *really* blue. I remember enough high school science to know that the color we think we see when we look at a large body of water is really just the sky reflecting off the water. It's an illusion of color more than it is color itself, but it's how we tap that illusion and make it our reality that fills our senses.

It's what we take in that counts—and it's what we put back out into the world.

That's how I came to feel about music—music of all shapes, sizes, whatever. It brought with it the illusion of belonging, and over time the illusion fell away and I finally counted.

See, besides not having a whole lot of friends when I was growing up, I also didn't have a big personality. My brother and sister were way older than me, and my mom was so old-school it's like she couldn't tap into whatever the hell was going on with me. Her ways were the ways of home—meaning Japan. My ways were the ways of here—meaning Newport Beach. That tug-and-pull, between how she was raised and how she was raising me, was at the heart of my childhood. She did her best and I was doing mine.

My father? He was more of a *presence* in my life than he was an actual presence, so it fell to me to mostly find my own way. It just worked out that music was that way. It opened up a path for me—a path I was blessed to discover . . . a path I continue to follow.

I figured things out, you know.

First music I heard that felt to me like it could be *my* music, where the artists seemed to be speaking to *me*, through *me*, was rap. I know I wrote earlier that I was into my brother's mod records, and I was, but that was *his* music. And like most kids in Newport Beach, I listened to Michael and whatever was playing on the radio, but that wasn't *my* music, so when I started to develop my own taste, when I finally connected to an artist or a beat or a sound on my own, it was all about Eazy-E and N.W.A and DJ Quik . . . that stuff just grabbed me by the balls, by the throat. It was different, difficult, diffuse. I couldn't tell you back then what I liked about it, but it spoke to me. In a fundamental way, almost visceral. It was angry, but it was the kind of angry where your back was against the wall and it felt like you were fucked but then you found a way to stand and be counted and make something happen for yourself. It wasn't about making trouble—it was about breaking ranks, finding ways to matter, and it opened up a kind of porthole I could climb through, into this whole other world, about as far removed from the lily-white streets of my neighborhood as the fucking moon.

Rap was my first crush, but I could never get close to it, always believed the music wasn't meant for me. I was put off, a little, by the lyrics. I wanted to find the poetry in what these guys were saying, the *truth* in what they were saying, so I'd actually grab a pen and a piece of paper and write down the lyrics. It was hard enough feeling like the only Asian kid in town, and now here I was inserting myself into the rap music scene, and last thing I wanted was for the other kids to dismiss me as some kind of poseur. Another last thing I wanted was to be counted out before I could be counted in. See, one of the things I was realizing was that music wasn't just about the beat or the lyric. You don't play this shit in a vacuum. You might zone out through your headphones, but what keeps you listening is that you're not the only one listening. I started to understand this even as a kid. The music was also about the community. It was about signing on and becoming a part of something.

Belonging—that's what I was after, after all. Soon, though, I started to realize that this wasn't *really* my music. Not yet, anyway. I was still on the outside looking in, but I wanted desperately to be on the inside looking out, so I'd study the lyrics, memorize them. I was determined to speak the language, and the lyrics were like my ticket inside. I swallowed every word, every beat, set myself up so I could spit them all back out in time with everyone else, and bounce and strut past the white picket fences of my neighborhood and rap about fuckin' tha police, about the cops fuckin' with me 'cause I was a teenager.

I moved like I was some kind of *playa* . . . because, in my head, that's what I was. That's what I wanted. Seems kinda funny to me now—kinda sad, kinda sweet—but I *owned* that shit. Didn't matter to me that I was this scrawny little Asian kid, looked nothing like the artists in these rap videos. I didn't even think about any of that, because the music put it out of my mind. I was swept up in it. But then at some point I had enough. The music, the rhymes, the beats . . . they filled me up to where I had no more room for any of it. I just wasn't *that guy*. Soon, I went from rap and discovered hardcore. The one led to the other. Because, let's face it, I didn't live in that world of rap or hip-hop. Took a while, and then I finally realized I could listen to rap but I couldn't *live* there, you know. First time I heard some straight-edge hardcore, though, I was hooked, thought I'd found a place for myself, at fucking last.

Straight-edge was a subgenre in the hardcore movement, took its name from a track by a band called Minor Threat. Do you know these guys? You should definitely seek them out, spend some time with them. Their music was all about the driving beat, the pulse, almost like punk, and there was still a sense of rebellion in their songs, except the message underneath the lyric was also about clean living, and community, and acceptance. Instead of just railing against the system, it offered a solution.

Listen up:

I'm a person just like you
But I've got better things to do
Than sit around and fuck my head
Hang out with the living dead

Pretty basic, right? But that was the essence of straight-edge—no room for doubt, no reading between the lines. The music itself was gritty and raw and in-your-face, shot through with pure energy, but there was something about the positive message that lit a small fire in me, fed my emerging sense of self. It didn't just give you permission to walk a straight line . . . it *expected* you to do so, made it like it was on you to lift people up, make the world a better place. I thought that was just awesome—to have to answer to the community. Keep in mind, this was going down in the years just after that crazy acid trip, when I was all about God and faith, and to me, just then, it all tied in. It was very different from the message at the heart of the rap music I'd been into, which was all about lifting yourself up, and doing right by *you*, maybe a little bit about you and your boys looking out for each other, so now I went out and copied down a whole new mess of lyrics, preaching about living clean, respecting the environment, promoting animal rights issues, whatever.

Here I could live. Here I could be myself, find myself.

Oh, and it wasn't enough for me to just listen to all this music. I was determined to soak it in through my pores . . . literally. First tattoo I ever got was a Gorilla Biscuits tat—an homage to their straight-edge anthem "Start Today," which was all about getting off your ass and living a life of purpose and meaning.

I was living this shit, breathing this shit. Wearing it on my heart. *Burning it into my skin.* Because when you're a kid, and you find a certain kind of music, a band or a movement or even just a snatch of lyric that touches you, it stays with you—like, forever. If it's authentic, it authenticates *you*. Doesn't have to be about music. You can find that authenticity, those points of connection, in movies, in books, in fashion, in art, in sports. For a time, I found it in those great Bruce Lee movies we used to watch over and over on video. For an Asian kid growing up in a white-bread community, Bruce Lee was like a lifeline. Can't overstate his influence—he put it out there that anything was possible. You didn't see too many Asian faces popping in our popular culture back then. You still don't. But Bruce Lee broke all those barriers. Bruce Lee let it be known that there was a place for us Asian kids.

All we had to do was find it.

Meanwhile, I had my few friends. By the time I got to middle school, high school, I had a small collection going. We were outliers, mostly. We were connected by our love of music, by the straight-edge hardcore scene, by skateboarding, by snowboarding . . . soon enough, by girls—although for me girls came later. Sometimes those lines of connection would cross, and there'd be a couple of us linked in a couple different ways, but for the most part I was bouncing between groups, fitting myself in wherever I could . . . always looking, looking, looking to find my Bruce Lee moments so I could stand and be counted.

We were little anarchists, some of us. We wouldn't make *serious* trouble, because that would cut against the straight-edge credo, but we would push the borders of what was considered acceptable behavior. I guess we could never quite find a place for ourselves in the comfortable middle, so we lived in the extremes, off to the side. One of the crazy things we did as kids was roof-hop across the whole neighborhood. It's a pretty descriptive term. We'd put camo makeup on our faces, put on some camo gear, climb up on some poor sucker's roof, and hop from house to house, building to building, up and down the block. The deal was you had to jump from roof to roof without touching the ground—and, hopefully, without busting up your ankles. Best

I can recall, no one was ever seriously hurt, although we did catch some shit for it when one of our moms found out what we were up to.

Once, when my hormones finally kicked in and I had the nerve to maybe do something about it, I set up a full drum kit on the front lawn of this girl I really liked. Her name was Jessica, and I parked myself right under her window and started playing. Middle of the fucking night. At least John Cusack did Ione Skye's neighbors the courtesy of firing up his boom box at a decent hour in *Say Anything*, that great Cameron Crowe movie. Here in real life—in *my* real life—I wasn't that considerate. Somebody turned on the lights, and I heard a bunch of yelling, and I tore ass out of there. I had some of my friends helping me out on that one, and they were on their instruments, and we all grabbed our gear and disappeared into the night.

When I ran into Jessica in the hall at school a couple days later, I asked her what she thought of our music.

She said, "Wait, that was you?"

I nodded.

She said, "You guys, like, suck."

She was right. We, like, did.

But we didn't give a shit. We just wanted to make some noise of our own, and that's all it was at first . . . *noise*. We taught ourselves to play by mimicking the bands we'd go to see. Whatever instrument we could get our hands on, that was what we played, so I was on drums for a while. I played some guitar. I sang. We taught ourselves, taught each other, swapped these little tricks we discovered. None of us knew what the fuck we were doing, but we found our way . . . eventually.

I played in a bunch of different bands—really, it was mostly the same people, moving in and out of what we were doing, depending on who was around. Sometimes we'd slap a new name on what we were doing, just because there was someone new on guitar or vocals. Sometimes a name didn't feel right for a show we were about to play—like at a Battle of the Bands night at school—so we switched it up, went with whatever we thought was cool at the time. One of our earliest lineups, and one of the most enduring, played under the name Goodhue, and I mention it here because it fits with the theme of this book. The name was in honor of our ceramics teacher, Mr. Goodhue, who was this buttoned-down old hippie we all thought was chill. A couple of us were in his class, and the name kind of popped. We liked it because it was our own little inside joke, but also because it played with the idea of the colors in our lives, all the different shades there are to humanity, to our moods, to the tint of our days.

Good. Hue.

You know, I think I like the name more now than I did then. I didn't understand all those layers as a kid, didn't get all those meanings. No way I could know at the time that with that name I was speaking into my future, and tapping the source, and celebrating the electric blue of a clear sky, the murky blue reflected off the deepest part of the ocean, the hopeless blue of the puppy love that left me banging on those skins on Jessica's front lawn at two o'clock in the morning.

Funny how when you move around the neighborhood—bouncing from rooftop to rooftop, banging out noise on some girl's front lawn— it feels to you like you know everything, but in reality you don't know shit. Back then, it didn't really matter what we knew, what we didn't know. My thing was all about finding a place for myself. I didn't like who I was, where I was coming from. I didn't like being different. And get this: not only were there just a few other Asian kids, there were just a couple other *boys*, so the odds were already stacked against me, but then I was so different from the other boys it's like I was in my own separate category. When I was super-little, I would eat lunch by myself, and that feeling stuck to me. It became my mind-set. Alone, isolated . . . that was how I looked out at the world, how I thought the world looked back at me. I was the kid whose mom packed him these weird little rice balls for lunch. I'd eat them at home all the time—*loved* them, actually— but it was embarrassing as hell to unwrap one of those suckers, with the funky bonito flakes making it look like the slivers of katsuobushi she'd rolled into them were slithering around.

The other kids would look at what I was eating and recoil. They'd shout, "Oooh, he's eating worms! Look at Aoki, he's eating worms!"

That kind of shit, it stays with you. You grow up eating this fucked-up food, looking oddly different, always feeling out of place, and you convince yourself the girls in your class won't like you because you have slanted eyes and your hair's not blond, and you start to feel separate. You move around like you are somehow *other* or *less than*.

And, so, you are . . .

Music was like the antidote—the great equalizer! It presented me with all these safe harbors, communities of people who didn't give a shit what I looked like or what I ate for lunch. I just wanted to slip into the background, make it so nobody even knew I was there, that's all. Told myself that since I couldn't find myself where I was, I would lose myself in the music and land someplace else. That was the plan.

Later, I'd learn that what I was seeking was a very Japanese ideal. It came from a place deep in the culture, so it must have been hardwired into my DNA, only I didn't really understand it until I was in college, studying the history of World War II. I wanted to learn what it was like for the Japanese prisoners in the internment camps, and what I found interesting was that they were endlessly obedient. There was no uprising, no rebellion. There were no walkouts. There was hardly a voice raised in protest . . . because that's just not the Japanese way.

In Japanese culture, nobody wants to stand out. My mother was that way, moving around our plain-vanilla community in Newport Beach, careful not to call attention to our little family. My father . . . not so much. He was a different sort of Asian, wasn't cut from traditional Japanese cloth. He was a tough old bird—hard, in the ways of the traditional Japanese father. But he also craved attention. His restaurants, his speedboat racing, his thrill-seeking adventures, they were all about standing out, not fitting in.

In this way, I guess, he was an outlier, too. He was different, other . . . and here I catch myself wishing we could have been different in the same ways. At the same time. Under the same roof.

This disconnect between Japanese traditions and how I was raised came to me again recently when I was touring Japan. We took a day off from the tour to create a show for a YouTube channel with a group of professional soccer players. The idea was we would kick soccer balls into a series of holes that were part of a giant target. The producers arranged for a bunch of people to stand behind the target and poke their faces through the holes, making them targets within the target. An announcer introduced the segment with a very famous saying from Japanese culture—loosely translated, it meant that whenever you see someone's head sticking out, you're supposed to bash it in.

This was us doing our part, bashing those faces in.

Anyway, that was the idea behind this whole piece, to send a soccer ball directly into the faces of these people who dared to stand out, because in Japan no one is meant to stand out. We're all in the same soup together . . . that's the ideal, because there's no room in traditional Japanese society for individuality. Everyone is the same. That's why there's no Japanese history of protest. You're meant to stay in line and keep your head down, go about your business.

And, whatever you do, you're not meant to make any noise.

Fuck that, right?

Music gave me permission to kick up some dust. I started going to a bunch of hardcore shows in dingy halls, along with a mob of mostly teenagers. Most of these venues were old punk clubs, and there was graffiti all over the walls, and it was super-dark, and everything smelled like beer and vomit and cat piss.

But it was cool. Hell, yeah . . . it was cool.

First couple shows, though, I kinda hung back, on the fringes. I was afraid to get in there and mix it up. People were moshing, and crowd-surfing, all these bodies colliding in a cramped, sweaty space. Everybody seemed to know one another, and I wasn't cool with these people. They didn't know me. Nobody knew me. I mean, I sometimes had my few friends with me, but it felt to us like we were crashing someone else's party. Still, I was drawn to that teeming crowd, pressed close to the stage. Wasn't exactly a full-on mosh pit, but it was calling to me, only I couldn't push my way in there until I could pass myself off as genuine. There was no way to know *all* these people and make myself feel comfortable around them, but I wanted them to at least get *the idea* of me. I wanted them to see me as the real deal, and I got it into my head that the way to be taken seriously at these shows was to know all the lyrics, to learn everything I could about the bands I was seeing, to wear their T-shirts. To walk the walk, same way I did when I was listening to all that rap music a couple years earlier. I bought all the demos, vowed I would learn every fucking word of every fucking song, and that I would sing my little-kid heart out.

I needed to plug in and feel the energy. And do you know what? I felt alive when I went to these shows. I wasn't *just* fitting in—I was finding my way. The music gave me a sense of purpose, a feeling of self-worth, made me feel like I belonged.

Hey, I was exploring a new culture, and to immerse myself in it I needed the right tools. I needed to dress the part. So I went to work. By the next show, I pushed myself to the front of the stage. I was singing, screaming along with everyone else. Jumping up and down. Having a big old time—feeling outside myself a little bit. At one point, this body came bobbing by, his arms flailing, his torso slithering like a caught snake. All I could think in that moment was that I wanted to be *that guy*. I wanted to surf across this crowd like these good people had been put in place just to carry me away. Like that was their sole purpose in life. Like that was *my* sole purpose in life. I watched that guy do his thing and made him my fucking hero. He was living the life I wanted—totally free and uninhibited. And then, the arms that were holding him up and passing him along just kind of gave way, and the poor guy fell to the floor. It seemed to happen in slow motion. It ended up, the dude cracked his head open when he hit the floor, hard. There was blood everywhere, and he started having these weird convulsions. Everyone kind of backed off, signaled for help.

The band kept playing, and I retreated into the crowd and wondered how it was that you can feel so incredible one moment, so invincible, and it can all turn to shit in an instant.

And then, underneath all of *that*, I wondered how some guy could crack his head open and the world kept spinning, the music kept playing. How something so significant could also be so insignificant.

That whole time I was out there getting deep into the straight-edge hardcore scene, we were putting together our first couple Goodhue gigs—only to call them "gigs" was maybe overstating things a little. We mostly played at our drummer Dana's house, in his living room. I was playing bass and singing, and then after a while we switched it up and my friend Jim jumped on bass. Another buddy, Alex, was on guitar. My great friend Dan Sena wasn't *with* us, exactly. He was never part of the band, but he was always around, always available to help us out, share what he knew about music. He's still a great friend today—he was really the musician of the bunch, taught me how to play guitar, how to really *shred*, how to stand with a mic and sing.

It was Dan who taught me how to record on a TASCAM four-track recorder, which was really the genesis of my work as a producer. He turned me on to all these different ways to listen to a piece of music, and out of that I found the courage and motivation to come up with my own riffs and create my own song.

One of the things we figured out early on was we could maybe hide our shortcomings as musicians with the depth of feeling we'd put into our playing. We would get into it—you know, thumping the mics against our chests, holding 'em upside down and tipping our heads to the ceiling . . . cranking the volume. It was all about the performance, the energy.

First time we ever played in front of people was in Alex's living room. We thought it was cool because it was a sunken living room, so it's like we were in a performance pit. We set up right in front of the fireplace. I was nervous as hell, sweaty as hell. I wore a backwards baseball cap and a flannel shirt that was probably two sizes too big— that was the look. There were maybe eight or ten people there, including the guitarist's parents. The way I'm describing it, it might seem like more of a rehearsal than a performance—I mean, we were just playing in one of our living rooms. But this was the real deal to us. These eight or ten people had stopped what they were doing and gathered to see us. If it was a rehearsal, people would have been coming in and out of the room, wandering into the kitchen to get something to eat.

What's funny, looking back, is that I knew everyone in that room, and yet I was unable to make eye contact with anyone. I just kept looking across the room, toward the front door, focusing my eyes above the small crowd, which was really just four or five of our friends and Alex's parents, or maybe looking up at the ceiling. It's like I was scared to connect with anyone, other than through the music. Or maybe I was embarrassed, didn't want to see a look of disappointment in anyone's eyes—yeah, that's probably what it was.

We weren't into slapping labels on our music, but we thought of ourselves as an emo band. Whatever we played was filtered through a legit hardcore edge. We played a twenty-minute set. I was singing and yelling my ass off, but I wasn't *screaming* . . . there's a difference. There was some tonality to what I was putting out there, although to judge from the reaction we were getting from our friends in that living room, I'm not entirely sure they would have agreed with me. At some point, I started to think the gig was going south. We were maybe halfway through the songs we were planning to play. The couple friends who'd come to see us were losing interest. And Alex's parents were kind of looking at their watches, looking bored.

Before the show, I'd taken the time to teach a couple of my friends the lyrics to one of our songs—a song I'd written called "All for One," a straight-edge revival song. I didn't write the lyrics out or anything, just kind of walked them through it, went over it a time or two. And now, as we were slogging through this one song where it felt to me like we were losing the crowd, I kept thinking, *Just let me get to this song I taught my friends.* The song was all about brotherhood and community. It had a strong hook, and I reached for it like a lifeline.

And, hey, the whole set turned on the back of that one song. My friends were into it. The guys I'd taught it to did their jobs and came up to the mic and started singing along with me:

All for one, one and all,
You and me stand together or fall . . .

We were all jumping up and down, together, and all of a sudden the room didn't feel so empty. It meant the world to me, to have my boys singing along with me like that. Meant the world to all of us, really. We were knitted together by the music we were making, the music we were hearing. It was a sweet, sweaty, unifying thing. It told us we were not alone, but even more than that it allowed us to think we might be onto something. And I guess, in a way, we were.

For another early gig, we decided to play a shopping plaza called Triangle Square, in Costa Mesa. There was a movie theater there we all used to go to, and they had this open-air courtyard where they'd sometimes feature artists—jazz combos, singer-songwriters, whatever. We thought that would be a good place for us to play, only it never occurred to us that this was something we'd have to arrange with management. We didn't know you had to book the gig—we just thought it'd be like playing in our parents' living room. We brought our drums, our guitars, our mics and started setting up. We decided to hold the show at two o'clock in the morning. We actually gave this some thought, probably figured we wouldn't be bothering anybody else at that hour, and that the kids who wanted to come out to hear us play would be able to find us.

This time around, we were calling ourselves the Box Packers—don't know why, but we all liked the name, and we were thinking of it as a kind of side project. Goodhue was our regular gig, and this would be our little experiment, where we could try out new shit. We'd only played together as Goodhue a couple times, and already we needed to have a side project.

There's an awesome shot from that night of me on acoustic guitar, singing, with Dan on the drums and Jim on bass. The photo's interesting because it's the only evidence we have that anyone came out to see us that night—one of our friends had to have been there to snap the pic, right? There was also a cop, we all seem to remember, who came out at some point to chase us away and ask us what the hell we thought we were doing.

A couple months into this scene—playing, going to a bunch of different shows, big and small—I wasn't hanging back on the fringes anymore. When I was onstage, performing, I was making eye contact with people in the audience, and when I was in the audience, whipping myself into a small frenzy, I was making eye contact with the artists on stage. I took it all very seriously. I shed whatever pieces of self-consciousness I was holding on to, and jumped right into the mosh pit, became a crowd-surfing fiend. Whatever inhibitions I'd had going in, I let them go soon enough. The music brought it out of me. The lyrics brought it out of me.

I'd press myself to the front and sing along and hope like hell the singer would hand me the mic, let me do my thing. Every fucking show, I was prepared. There was this one band, Farside, they started to notice that I was down in front every time they played. They knew me as their biggest fan . . . and I guess I was. At one show, they called me up, brought me onstage, asked me to sing this song "Hero" with them.

I had that song *down*, motherfucker . . .

Here's a taste:

I want to be the hero
The one you've always dreamed of
I want to be the one to save the day again . . .

It was like getting called up to the front of the room by the teacher when you know all the material. I was good and ready. There's a picture from that night, too, with the whole band backing me, and it's one of my most treasured keepsakes. I pull it out from time to time and try to remember the awkward, searching kid I was, how eager I was to fit myself in to this new community, and how easily it all started to happen for me once I connected to the hardcore scene.

It was so *right there . . .*

DROP

I don't always look at the color of someone's eyes.

Anyway, it's not the first thing I notice.

Maybe that's because so many people I know hide their eyes behind a pair of shades, day or night, inside or out. Or they look away instead of right at you. But I think it goes to something deeper. I'll notice someone's clothes or their makeup or their hair—and I'll definitely check out their kicks!—but the eyes kind of disappear into the background for me . . . unless they're a striking shade, like a deep hazel, or an unusual green like you sometimes see in Sweden and Denmark. Then I'll stop and stare. But if they're brown, I might not even notice.

You'd think, with the way people shout about having blue eyes, or crushing on someone with blue eyes, I'd pay more attention. Western music is filled with the romantic notion of blue-eyed love. Rock, country, punk, hardcore . . . you've even got the Chairman of the Fucking Board, the entertainer who put my city on the map, Sinatra himself, known forevermore as Ol' Blue Eyes.

Remix all those songs, mash up all those messages and images, and what you come away with is the idea that when you look out at the world through a blue lens, the world smiles back. Hard. Funny thing, though: I've been told that you don't see blue eyes all that often in people from Japan. I'd never really noticed, but this is true, now that I think of it. Really, I can't think of anyone in my family with blue eyes. Can't think of any blue-eyed

Japanese heroes or leaders. In fact, most Asians are brown-eyed—but then, if you look at a lot of the cutting-edge art that's coming out of that part of the world, the blue-eyed ideal is very much a thing.

In Japanese anime art, for example, you'll often see heroes or heroines with blue eyes . . . and, say, yellow hair. Why is that, do you think? I have a theory, and it ties back to how traditional Japanese culture is rooted in conformity. We've been over this, yeah, but this is the ground I've walked my whole fucking life, so let's go over it again. In Japan, nobody wants to stand out, so we stand down. We keep quiet, dress quiet, live quiet, so when you look at anime you see that the characters with dark hair and dark eyes are the most common. Makes sense, right? But if you study it, do a quick survey, you'll also see that the characters with dark hair or dark eyes don't have a whole lot to do with the story that's being told. They're in a supporting role—meaning, in support of whatever or whoever is extraordinary.

Okay, so I'm generalizing here. It's not like I've done this comprehensive study, but follow my thought and see if you don't agree. In the world of anime, dark hair seems to represent the majority, the great many, while it's the exceptional characters that are drawn with yellow hair—signifying a special quality, perhaps—or bright green eyes, or whatever. You'll even see blue hair, from time to time, usually on a character with great strength or resolve. Red, purple, pink . . . you can probably do a whole thesis on the use of color in anime art and come up with character traits connected to every shade, every body part, and there in the background you'll find a crowd of everyday folks with their same-seeming hair, their same-seeming eyes.

But that's just fantasy, right? In our reality, only way we can look out at the world with blue eyes is to put on blue lenses. To think boldly, to grab at the idea that we're seeing the world with blue eyes. Because even as we seek to be different—in our art, in our dreams—we stay as we are, very much the same.

So what does this all mean? Fuck, I'm not even sure . . . but as long as I'm jumping to conclusions, I'll jump to this one: maybe, just maybe, the young Japanese artists breaking through the culture are looking to shed these old traditions. Maybe they're tired of standing down, tired of the ways their brothers and sisters have been made to stand down, and they want to push us to stand and be counted.

To stand out.

Better believe it, I can see these traditions fading at my shows, in the United States and all over the world. My Asian fans turn out in big numbers with brightly colored hair—lately, pink. They're wearing blue—like a bright neon. They're doing whatever they can to call attention to whatever it is they're into. They want to pop and sizzle and make an impression, to step from the background and stand front and center. So when I look out from the stage at that sea of bodies colliding in time to my music, dotted here and there with a mop of hair dyed a screaming shade of blue—the blue of nonconformity!—I know there's a young person beneath those bright colors hoping to make some serious noise.

Someone exceptional.

6

MINE TO KEEP

That TASCAM four-track recorder I wrote about earlier was like a gift from the music gods, a game-changer. I'd been writing songs in my bedroom, following a very basic power chord structure—just finding my way, you know. When I had something I liked, I'd invite my buddy Dan over and play it for him, and after a while he said I should get this recorder. I was decent enough on the drums, decent enough on guitar, on bass, on vocals, and his idea was I should put it all together and hear how it sounded. The way he described it made me think it would be like making a collage. He told me what to buy, said this TASCAM was the cheapest and most useful recording device on the market, so I went to my mother and told her about it.

I said, "Mom, you know I've been writing music, right?"

She said, "Yes, Steven. I know. I can hear you writing your music."

Funny thing—she didn't say that she was proud of me or excited for me that I was so into music. She didn't say that she *liked* what she was hearing, when I sat in my room all day playing the guitar. Wasn't like that with my mom. She'd always left me alone to do my thing, never really talked to me about music or any of the other things I was interested in—not because she didn't care, but because this was just her way. She was an independent soul, and she wanted me to be an independent soul, I guess. But I didn't have the money to buy this TAS-CAM unit, so I needed to bring her into my world a little bit. The recorder cost a couple hundred bucks, which might as well have been a couple thousand. So I told my mom what I would use it for, why I needed it, how important it was to me.

She just said, "Fine, let's go."

I'd never really asked for anything expensive before, and my mom could see how passionate I was about making and recording my own music, so she made it like it was no big deal—even though, to me, it was a *really* big deal.

Another funny thing: it never even occurred to me to ask my father. When we were together we were mostly in vacation mode, in family reunion mode, so I never wanted to have my hand out. He was generous with us kids when we were traveling or when he was visiting, but when it came to an allowance or giving me money for my day-to-day stuff, he wasn't part of my thinking. Whatever I needed, whatever I couldn't manage on my own with my various after-school jobs, I had to work it out with my mom.

You know how there are these turning points in your life, when everything that happens next falls from this one pivotal moment? Well, getting this TASCAM four-track was one of those moments. Without that TASCAM, there would be no Dim Mak, no Aoki's Playhouse, no career. We went that afternoon to a small little music shop where I knew they would have it, and my whole world changed when I brought that sucker home and took it out of the box. It didn't look like much—just a small gray console, about the size of a shoebox, with a row of mixing knobs along one side of the front panel and a slot for a standard cassette tape on the other.

I couldn't read or write music, so all the songs I'd been working on were bouncing around in my head, or maybe stored on one of the crude demos I was always making on an old cassette recorder. But I knew I had to try out my new toy, so I sat down and played this song I'd been working on called "Broken Heart." I recorded the guitar part, then I raced a couple houses over to our rehearsal space in my friend Dana's living room, where we had a drum kit all set up, and I recorded the percussion part. Then I shot back home and did the bass part and sang the vocal.

The lyric was simple: "Oh, you broke my heart. Oh, you broke my heart."

(Hey, what do you want from me? I was fifteen years old, had never even kissed a girl, didn't think I had a chance with any of the girls I liked, so this was me singing about my eternally broken heart.)

First call I made was to Dan—told him I had something I wanted to play for him and to hurry over. Wish I could say he was blown away by my song, but he wasn't the most effusive guy. Plus, the song wasn't very good. Only way it could blow you away was if you were a paper doll, listening in a stiff wind. Still, he was pumped—said, "You did it, man!"

Yep, I did it. Dan was right about that—I fucking did it. And, like I said, the song was probably horrible, my musicianship was probably horrible, but to me, just then, it was the best thing anyone had ever set down on tape. It was epic. Right away, my head filled with delusions of grandeur. I would put that song out, and I would get signed, and sell millions of records. I would tour all over the country, maybe even overseas. I was ready to go big.

Of course, that's not what happened. It's nowhere near what *should* have happened. But somehow the takeaway for me from Dan's grudging *what the hell*-type approval was that I could do anything. That *we* could do anything. And for no good reason beyond youthful enthusiasm and self-delusion, I went to bed that night dreaming of a career in the music business.

It was all so clearly within reach.

Next day, I played the song for my friends in the band, and they brought me back down. One of them said, "Holy shit, this is bad." Everyone agreed . . . myself included. But then we listened to the track again and our drummer Dana said, "I know what you were going for there. I think I can do better. Let me try." Our guitarist, Andreas, same thing. And out of that I was able to take out my TASCAM recorder and start in again on the song. Jim was already crushing it on bass, so of course he could play it better than me, but it took this group deconstruction for me to see the songs I was making for what they were. Over time, I decided I would only do the vocal parts, because my friends were so much more capable on their instruments. I could play, some, enough for you to recognize there was a song somewhere in there among the notes, but the process allowed me to compartmentalize the music I was trying to create.

What ended up happening was that I started recording more and more of my own music and sharing it with this fluid collection of friends in this fluid collection of bands, and my TASCAM four-track became this tremendous collaborative tool. It really inspired me, and because I couldn't read or write music I would communicate my ideas for these songs through the recordings I made on my own at home. I started to realize that I didn't need to know how to *write* music in order to *create* music, and it was a liberating thing.

College had always been a given for me. Music was all I really cared about, but in my own way I'd been an okay student in high school. If I was interested in the class, in the material, I did well. If I wasn't interested, I struggled—that's how it goes for a lot of kids, right? I liked to read, to learn about new discoveries, different ways of life. I was curious about the world, but I didn't always see the point of studying for a test just to prove to some professor that I understood the material. Either you learned this shit or you didn't; either it meant something to you or it didn't. But that's not how the game is played, right? You have to show a certain mastery of a subject in order to get to the next level, which in this case meant earning a degree and heading out into the world.

For a while, it was also a given that whatever course of study I chose to pursue, whatever career path I might follow, it could lead me eventually to Benihana. Wasn't any kind of done deal, but going into the family business was always a prospect. I'd worked in the kitchen a couple summers for my brother Kevin—in Texas, in Hawaii, where he was managing my father's restaurants. I didn't love it, but I didn't hate it—something to think about, that's all.

My father was an interesting guy. He never really talked about this stuff with us kids. Like with my music, he never mentioned that he played bass in a band when he was in high school. Looking back, that would have been good to know—we could have maybe connected on this level. And the thing of it is, we never really connected on a Benihana level, either. He never came out and told me there was a place for me at the table if I wanted to work with him. That was Kevin's deal—that was the Japanese way. Kevin was the firstborn son, so he was the natural apprentice, the heir apparent, whatever. It was embedded in the culture, very traditional. I wasn't even Son #2—that honor went to my brother Kyle. I was just the kid brother, Son #3, so I'd work summers peeling onions, doing assembly-line stuff in the kitchen. If I thought about my future at all in those days, I guess I thought I'd study business or marketing, maybe go to work for my father in the office and not in the restaurant. I just didn't see myself in the kitchen, in the front of the house, working restaurant hours.

One thing my father always made clear, though: nothing would be handed to me. If I wasn't suited to the business, there'd be no place for me. It wasn't any kind of birthright, at least not for me. Kevin was the one being groomed to take over someday. The rest of us could either work there or not . . . take it or leave it . . . it didn't much matter.

I went off to school without a clear path in mind—that is, without a clear *professional* path. The rest of it, I thought I had the next four years to figure it all out. I wasn't giving up on music just yet. I knew it would continue to be a big part of my life, but I also knew that in some ways it was just a placeholder for the direction that would find me later on. I ended up majoring in Women's Studies, which exposed me to all kinds of critical and creative thinkers and activists, and turned me on to philosophy and literature—a tremendous grounding for a student of the world, but not exactly a foundation for a future titan of the restaurant business.

It was also a kind of neutralizer for the traces of religion I continued to carry all through high school. Yeah, I might have "found" God on my little-kid acid trip, but I didn't exactly grab on with both hands. My passion fell away over time, and by the time I started reading all these great writers in college, my interests were much more rooted in the real than in the surreal. I was drawn to critical thinkers, activists, critics . . . material connected to the here and now, ideas intended to shape a better world. In my emerging sense of self, it no longer made sense to live in fear of the unknown when I could be chasing all these knowable, palpable truths instead.

On the music front, I'd gone from those delusions of grandeur that hit me after I'd made that first TASCAM recording to recognizing that I'd probably never make it as a musician. You know, I'd been in a bunch of bands, and I loved it—but, end of the day, I was starting to think I was a failure as a musician. My bands never played for more than thirty, forty people. We never made the kind of noise you need to make to get noticed. So I was starting to take the hint, you know.

I wasn't always the most pragmatic person in the room, but you didn't have to beat me over the head to get me to see what was clearly right in front of me.

For the time being, though, the music was stuck to me. Mine, someone else's . . . whatever. And it's not like you were meant to be making money off the transaction. The artists I loved and admired weren't in it to make money. They were in it to feed the community, to feed their souls. It was all so raw, so pure. That's what I so dearly loved about the hardcore scene—the music stood for itself. That was the ideal. If you were out there trying to sell, sell, sell, the fans would see right through you. That wasn't what hardcore was about.

Wasn't what *I* was about.

I wanted to immerse myself in the culture, to taste whatever I could before I had to suck it up and get a real job. That's where college came in. I'd find something that interested me and get to work on it, and underneath all of that I'd buy myself another four years to play my music and soak up the vibe. I applied to all the UC schools but decided on UC Santa Barbara because it was close to the small town of Goleta, California. That's where Ebullition Records was based, where the label's influential zine *HeartattaCk* was published. Goleta was the hardcore hub, our own little mecca, and *HeartattaCk* was like the Bible for hardcore fans. Everyone I knew read each issue cover to cover, as soon as it came out. It talked about all my favorite bands, all my favorite artists . . . and I read every word.

When I looked at a map and saw that Goleta was basically a suburb of Santa Barbara, I knew that was where I was going. The town was like a magnet, and it was all because of Ebullition, and this guy Kent McClard, who ran the place. One thing you should know: I collected records in those days the way other kids collected comic books. Every single release. Every single artist. And I'm not talking about major-label shit—no, I only cared about these hardcore indie labels. Revelation Records, Ebullition . . . whatever these guys put out, I would snatch it up, starting when I was still in high school, scraping together whatever money I could find from all of my summer jobs and side hustles. It almost didn't matter to me who the artist was on the record. I knew the labels more than I knew the artists, but then of course if the labels I cared about got behind a certain band, then I *had* to go see them.

The one fed the other.

I had all these great collections, and they had to be complete collections. It was like an obsession. If I was missing Vermiform Number Seven, say, I just had to have it. That was Sam McPheeters's label, and I chased down that one missing record for the longest time. I didn't even know who the artist was—it didn't matter. I just had to have it. Once, I drove all the way to Moorpark, way down in Ventura County, just to see this one guy who had these rare pressings. Don't know what I was expecting, because he wasn't offering any of his records for sale, but I just wanted to breathe in all that vinyl, to see what I had to do to get to his level.

Anyway, it would bring me this tremendous sense of fulfillment to complete each little collection, from each independent label I was following. A sense of accomplishment. And I've got to confess, I'm still this way about the things that matter to me. I can get crazy-obsessive when I'm into something—sneakers, video games . . . even Japanese teas! These days, it's mostly about art. I find an artist I like, someone who speaks to me, and it's like I have to corner the market. The way I'm wired, it's like there's something in me that won't let me feel whole until I complete the set.

The work doesn't speak to me in a small, sweet voice—I need to hear the whole fucking chorus, big as the wild blue yonder.

One of the first things I did when I got to school was trek to Goleta, to see if maybe there was a place for me at Ebullition. I was down to sweep the floors, answer the phones . . . anything to be invited inside that world. Kent McClard was an intimidating character. He was only about ten years older than me, in his late twenties, but I looked up to him like he was some kind of god. I read everything he wrote—and most of *HeartattaCk* was him riffing on the scene, on all these different artists, on popular culture.

Dude had some things on his mind, let's say that.

That first visit to the Ebullition office was another one of those turning-point moments for me, right up there with getting that TAS-CAM four-track. Same deal: without Ebullition, there would be no Dim Mak, no Aoki's Playhouse, no career . . . that's how important this was for me.

The office itself was just an old warehouse, with cardboard boxes piled everywhere. Wasn't any kind of temple of hardcore, like I'd been expecting. And as for Kent, who'd built this empire, he was just this cynical, sarcastic guy, seemed to like to bust people's balls and give them a hard time.

There was only one person in the office other than Kent—a young woman named Lisa Oglesby, who in a lot of ways was the glue of the operation, the Chief Everything Officer. It was hard to reconcile this grand image I'd had in my head of what this place would be like with this shabby, shitty reality. But that's how the world works, right? You peek behind the curtain, you see how the sausage is made, and you lose whatever illusions you've been carrying around in your head.

Somehow, I convinced Kent to take me on as an intern. I started hanging around as much as I could, sorting records, stuffing mailers . . . doing a little bit of everything. Eventually, Kent let me review some records for *HeartattaCk*, and it's like I'd died and gone to heaven. Seriously. There were my initials, right there in my favorite zine. You'd just flip to the back of the review section and see that "SA" was "Steve Aoki." It was the coolest feeling in the world, to be attached to the scene in this way, to be *credentialed* in this way. After a while I became like the go-to reviewer for other zines, records, demos, shows— whatever nobody else wanted to review, I would take it on.

Meanwhile, my college career wasn't exactly off to the best start. I was living on the seventh floor of my freshman dorm with a guy who listened to Howard Stern every morning. Nothing against Howard Stern, but in those days he only came on at six o'clock in the morning, and my asshole roommate didn't seem to understand the concept of headphones. I didn't have it in me to say anything, though—a part of me still felt like the fish out of water I'd always been, so I let my room-mate step on me in this way, to where I'd get out of bed every morning feeling anxious and sleep-deprived and pissed at myself for not stand-ing up to him. People who know me today might not recognize me in this story, but I was a shy kid. Awkward. Confrontation wasn't my thing, and even when I did find the courage to make myself heard, the slightest pushback would suck the courage right back out of me. As a Japanese kid who never really felt like he fit in, I'd spent so long *stand-ing down* I didn't have it in me to *stand up*.

Not yet, anyway.

After a while, I moved out of the dorm and into a vegan co-op called Dashain House. We were a bunch of budding political activists, a weird collection of hippies and straight-edge kids. Dashain was the name we'd given to a pet rat that lived there, was kind of like our mas-cot, and it was there that I started putting on shows, just like we used to do back in Newport Beach, playing in our friends' living rooms to ten, twenty, thirty people, only now we were getting bands with a little bit of a following. Jimmy Eat World played one night in our kitchen . . . to about twenty people! It was insane. Jim Adkins and them had such a blast, they came back and played a second time. Can't tell you what a trip that was for us—for *me!*—to get these guys to play at our little vegan co-op, because they were huge! And we didn't even have a stage, or a decent place for them to set up, but they were totally into it.

We had a ton of bands come through Dashain House—a couple

shows a week. At first, it was just me and my friends and whatever band we had going at the time, and out of that we started booking our friends' bands, and then friends of friends, but eventually we started attracting artists from these influential indie labels. It all happened organically, and along the way I started drifting from playing my own shows to promoting all these other shows, like it was the most natural thing in the world for me to be doing.

I wasn't the only guy on campus staging these homegrown hardcore shows, though. I had a group of good friends doing the same thing over at their house, a much smaller place that had been dubbed the Pickle Patch by my buddy Mike O'Brien. O.B.—that's what everyone called him—was way into pickles, and he had this idea that the house was like a pumpkin patch, but with pickles. It was just a stupid little inside joke, made no sense, but the name stuck, and while we were putting on our own pop-up shows at Dashain House, named for a rat, these guys were putting on slightly bigger shows at *their* house, named for a cucumber.

I had another buddy at the Pickle Patch named Mike Phyte, and he was really my closest hardcore friend, and when a spot opened up in the house he asked me to move in and start putting on these shows with him full-time. I jumped at the chance—another one of those turning points for me, because the Pickle Patch shows we'd go on to stage together were legendary. Once again, without Pickle Patch, there would be no Dim Mak, no Aoki's Playhouse, no career.

(Are you sensing a pattern?)

Here's when things *really* started to happen for me . . . when *all* these turning-point moments seemed to come together. I was nineteen years old, and before the start of my junior year I went with my band This Machine Kills for a tour of Japan. Actually, to call it a "tour" is probably a stretch, but we went with our instruments and a loose plan to play a bunch of shows. Actually, too, there were a couple of these

Japanese "tours" in there, and they all kind of run together in my memory. One thing is clear, though: we didn't have any money, and it wasn't likely that we were going to make all that much of it while we were over there, but on one of these trips at least I knew my mom very quietly paid for our plane tickets. I knew at the time that she'd paid for *my* ticket, but she never said anything about paying for the other guys in the band—I'd always just thought they'd dipped into their own pockets or hit up their own parents for their airfare. But money wasn't the first thing on my mind in those days. Wasn't second or third, either.

Like I said, our whole deal was to feed the community, which in turn would feed us. That was the hardcore creed, but here it could only cover us with a place to crash and a meal every here and there. It was the *getting* from here to there that we couldn't afford, so my mom just took care of it all for us, without really calling our attention to what she was doing. She even hooked me up with a train pass so I could travel around the country.

I'd been to Japan before, but only with my family. This was my first time traveling alone, and we bounced from city to city, taking in all these hardcore shows, playing wherever we could. We'd set up some shows beforehand, and added a bunch of others on the fly. I knew a couple Japanese words and phrases, but I mostly got by on English. Along the way, I splintered off from the group and did some traveling on my own. I met up with a post-hardcore band called Envy. They knew my name from my initials-only signature in *HeartattaCk*—that was the power and reach of that zine back then. I gave the lead singer, Tetsuya, a copy of our This Machine Kills demo, and he seemed to dig it. Out of that, he offered to do a split seven-inch recording with us, and I was fucking floored. I mean, Envy was a big, big deal, and here they wanted to share a sliver of their spotlight with our shitty little band. They wanted to share the stage with us, too—they ended up inviting us to open for them at a couple dates, so we hit the road with them, traveling all over the country with our train passes.

I was so fucking thrilled to be able to tap into the Japanese music scene in this way. It was more than I could have ever expected.

I came back to Santa Barbara just before the fall semester and settled into my new Pickle Patch digs. The house was cut up into four apartments. Apartment A was me and the Pickle Patch guys: Mike O'Brien, Mike Phyte, and Andy Fraire, another Dashain housemate. I shared a room with Phyte, and another friend of ours, Brett Bezsylko, quickly joined our little circus, taking O.B.'s spot. In Apartment B, there were a couple writers from *HeartattaCk*, including Kent Mc-Clard and Brett Hall, who was also the guitarist in This Machine Kills. In Apartment C, there was Ebullition's "CEO," Lisa Oglesby, and Leslie Kahan, one of the main *HeartattaCk* writers.

Right there in that one building you had a lot of the main influencers of the local hardcore scene, so it felt to me like we were at the center of everything—and we were.

Very quickly, the Pickle Patch became one of the most important music venues on the West Coast. Same way I'd come to town thinking Goleta was a kind of hub for hardcore music, that's the way people started thinking of the Pickle Patch. Its reputation had nothing to do with size or seating capacity, and everything to do with the vibe and the cred that came with it. It got to where we started hearing from these major artists we all looked up to, and their managers were desperate to get them a date on our calendar—thinking, you know, that we were some kind of big-time venue—and then the guys in the band would show up in our living room and think they were being punked. They'd look around and flash each other these incredulous looks, like they couldn't believe this crappy little apartment was an important venue.

Here's a good example of how big we were—and it's tied to a group that never even made it to our living room. I still remember when we booked Refused, one of my favorite bands of all time, but they broke up before they ever got to do the show. Years later, they got back together for a reunion tour, and I flew to San Francisco to check them out. In the past ten years, I'd say I've traveled to another city to see a band on only two occasions. The other time was to see Drive Like Jehu, another of my favorite bands, from San Diego. But this one time I hopped on a plane to see Refused was a revelation. They'd put out this great album, *The Shape of Punk to Come*—widely considered one of the greatest hardcore albums ever, ever, ever. And I was still a little bummed, even after all these years, that they never made it to our living room, but then I got to their reunion show, and between songs they started talking about the Pickle Patch. It was upside down—almost like *they* were bummed they never got to play there. And now here they were, at this sold-out show in San Francisco, telling this story about how they were trying to get to this one gig at the Pickle Patch, making it sound like Madison Square Garden.

One of the biggest bands to ever do a Pickle Patch show was At the Drive-In—one of the craziest live bands, probably one of the most influential bands on the post-hardcore scene. They had this album out at the time called *In/Casino/Out*, and their manager was hitting us up constantly. We were so stoked they wanted to play at our place, because they were huge. It was a major get for us. But then the manager got there ahead of the show and said, "Are you fucking kidding me? I can't fit thirty people in here."

I said, "This is the Pickle Patch, man. This has always been the Pickle Patch. Don't know what to tell ya."

He said, "I can't put my band in here."

I said, "Dude, your guys are here. They want to play. We've got all these kids here, dying to see them play."

We went back and forth for a while, but At the Drive-In ended up playing and putting on a sick, sick show. Cedric Bixler-Zavala, the lead singer, was climbing all over the furniture, and our friends were jumping from the staircase rail into the small crowd, bouncing all over the place. It was fucking nuts . . . but then, that's what it was like every time we put on a show. Twenty shows a month, on average. Four bands a night. Do the math—over the course of the academic year, that came to over three hundred bands, filling our tiny living room with sound and fury and legend.

What was so incredible about what we were doing at the Pickle Patch was that the place was such a shithole. Our living room was about the size of a small studio apartment, with a ratty old carpet pocked by stains and cigarette burns and tears. The rug was filthy, frayed at the edges, foul. There was a shotgun kitchen with a peeling linoleum floor. And a single nasty-ass toilet that was always busted, always disgusting. If a building inspector had ever come by to check the place out, I'm sure we would have been in violation of a couple dozen codes. The coolest thing about our setup was the staircase that ran alongside one wall, a great spot to hang and watch the band, or to dive into the crowd.

Hot Water Music, Cave In, Ten Yard Fight . . . all these amazing artists would shoehorn themselves into this small space and play their asses off, and even if they were scratching their heads on the way in, wondering what the hell they were doing there, by the time they finished their forty-minute sets they were almost always stoked, and asking when they could come back. We very quickly became a magnet for underground shows on the West Coast—a must-stop on the circuit. I don't know that there's a good equivalent for the place we occupied on the cultural scene during our brief shining moment, but some people compared our rep in the music business to places like the Roxy, in Los Angeles, or CBGB in its funky-frantic heyday, in New York, or 924 Gilman, in San Francisco. It was *the* place to be, where the music happened.

Obviously, we couldn't afford to pay these bands—we were just a bunch of college kids, making it up as we went along. But we gave them the door, usually at five dollars a head, and if they wanted to sell vinyl, T-shirts, or other merch, they could stake out a small corner of the apartment and set up a table.

They didn't play for the money. They played for the moment.

For a hot while, the Pickle Patch was the epicenter of our pulsing hardcore community, a glorious combustion of sound and energy . . . and I was honored to be a part of that. And it's important that I emphasize that I was *just* a part of that. We were a collective. The Pickle Patch had been going on before I got there. I didn't start it . . . I didn't name it . . . but once I signed on, I kind of helped it along. There was a group of us working it, lining up bands, setting up the equipment, promoting the shows, making sure the toilet wasn't permanently stopped up or we didn't blow a fuse. It was a total team effort, and it didn't have a thing to do with making money.

Oh, there was probably money to be made—but none of us really had that killer business instinct . . . and even if we had, we didn't see the honor in making a buck off these bands, off our friends, off the music we loved. It would have been inauthentic, shitty. It all went back to the hardcore culture. The music was meant to lift you up, not pinch a couple bucks from your pocket. It was real, honest, and to us this meant there had to be a kind of hard line between art and commerce.

That didn't keep us from building our own little sideline businesses alongside these Pickle Patch shows, but they were built on a nonprofit model. Part of the reason for that was that we had no idea what the hell we were doing, no idea how to run a business, so any kind of profit was always just out of reach, but it had mostly to do with the fact that it wasn't cool to monetize what we were doing. In my head, at least, it was all about sharing our passion for this music, supporting our fellow artists, enriching the community.

The first one of us to make the leap from our living room into the wide, wide world of the record business was my great pal Mike Phyte, who started his own label, Phyte Records. Mike had already graduated by this point and was working full-time as the manager at the local Kinko's, so he used the copy machines there to print the jackets and liner notes for the small press runs he had going for a couple bands. That's also where we ran off all the flyers we made to promote our Pickle Patch shows, which we'd staple to light poles all around campus, tuck beneath the windshield wipers on the cars in the parking lots, tape to the windows of local store owners who wanted to support their community.

I was inspired by what Mike was doing and decided to start a label of my own. What's interesting to me, looking back, is the way all of these turning-point moments came together when I was nineteen: Pickle Patch, the tour of Japan, starting my own label. I called the label Dim Mak, a martial arts term that translates as "touch of death." The name just kind of called to me, I guess because I'd always idolized Bruce Lee, put him on his own damn pedestal, and those old movies really inspired me when I was a kid. The whole idea that you could kill someone with a very specific, very purposeful touch had always struck me as violently romantic. It was personal and impersonal. The phrase referred to the ancient technique of targeting a spot on the body—the temple, the heart—and I was fascinated by the subtlety and poetry of that kind of evil. It put it out there that death can find you in the unlikeliest ways, when you least expect it. Don't know what the hell the phrase had to do with hardcore other than the fact that it was *hardcore*—but, hey, it was my fucking label, and I could call it whatever the hell I wanted.

First artist I "signed" to Dim Mak was my friend Dan Sena, from Newport Beach. I put that word in quotes because I think our signing ceremony consisted of a handshake. He had a band called Stick Figure Carousel, and they'd yet to record anything, and I was dying to put something out, so it was a good fit all around.

My idea with this label was that it would be another way for me to support these artists who didn't have an outlet. It would be an extension of what we were doing with our Pickle Patch shows. I didn't have any money, wasn't any kind of record executive, not by any stretch. I was working a bunch of minimum wage–type jobs—working as a telemarketer in a local call center, delivering greasy food on my bicycle—just to cover my expenses. I had exactly $400 in my bank account.

Dan was my good friend, and he was ridiculously talented, and I wanted to push him along however I could. Dan had a couple new songs he wanted to record with his new band, but I wasn't confident enough in what I was doing to go it alone, so I got these two friends of mine to partner with me on this first pressing—John and Gabe Bowne, twin brothers I'd known since high school. They knew Dan's music, knew he had talent, and they'd started a label of their own called Bastille Records. They'd already released a seven-inch, so they were way ahead of the curve compared to me.

We ended up splitting the costs three ways. John and Gabe each put up $400 to match the money I had to invest, and we set about it. I think it cost $200 to record Dan's two songs—"For the Kids" and

"Moribund Summer." The rest of the money went to pressing, packaging. It was a do-it-yourself operation, but it still cost money. We decided to do a limited-edition run of 600 copies. We made the sleeves ourselves at Kinko's. (Shout-out to Mike Phyte, who looked the other way when we invaded his copy center!) We got special paper, and made diecuts for the sleeves, and folded everything by hand.

I had this idea that in every Dim Mak release I'd have a kind of signature element in the packaging, something to reflect what was going on with me at the time. It didn't have to be about the songs we were putting out or the artists we were promoting, but I wanted there to be a throughline connecting all these hoped-for Dim Mak releases. I was thinking back to the artists and labels I'd collected so passionately back in high school, and I wanted to speak in some way to the kid I was then, desperate to belong, so I designed this endpiece as part of our liner notes. It was my way of putting my own stamp on each release, a little something of myself. I learned about graphic design and came up with this cool feature that really popped on the sleeve. I called it "Hearts and Minds," and for this very first Stick Figure Carousel pressing—Dim Mak #1!—I reached for a quote from my father:

"If you're afraid of dying, you're afraid of living."

Wasn't something he ever said to me, but I'd seen it in some article, and it made an impression. My idea with this Hearts and Minds element was to honor the people who had an impact on me, in one way or another, and after this quote from my dad I'd end up using quotes from people like Angela Davis, Huey P. Newton, Mumia Abu-Jamal, Gloria Anzaldúa, and on and on. Activists, poets, artists . . . whoever was speaking *to* me at that time in my life, I would have them speak *through* me with this little stamp I designed into each package.

With that first Stick Figure Carousel release, we took those 600 copies and started selling them at shows, from the trunk of our car. I placed an ad in *HeartattaCk* that cost us $35. We sold the records for $3.00, kept the money in this little piggy bank we carried around with us. The hard cost on each record was about $2.00, but that didn't account for the studio time or the cost of the paper we used for the sleeves, so we were making about 75 cents per record. Plus, we had to give a whole bunch of them away, just to call attention to what we were doing, so it's not like this was any kind of moneymaking operation.

But do you know what? It wasn't a money-*losing* operation, either, so I decided to do a second release. This time, I would go it alone. For my second release, I tapped this exciting band out of San Diego called I Wish I. (Cool name, right?)

I reached out to Dan again for my third release, only by this time he was playing with a new band called Give Until Gone, and for this one I decided to put the music on CD. I was experimenting, playing with the formula, and I thought that since CDs would be cheaper than a vinyl pressing, there'd be more money left over if we sold through, but what I hadn't counted on was that CDs weren't nearly as collectible as vinyl. This was just me misreading the market, looking at what things cost instead of what they represented. I should have known better—me, of all people. That fifteen-year-old kid in Newport Beach, feeling a little outside the mainstream? He wasn't going out of his way to buy a CD, which can be mass-produced and reproduced until it loses its authenticity. Yeah, you could get the music out there in a cost-effective way, but it wasn't what I wanted to be doing. I wanted to re-create the excitement I felt collecting all that great indie vinyl, with the records hand-numbered. There's just something about a limited-edition record that gets me going, you know, so out of that one little misstep I told myself I'd never make a decision based solely on the numbers. The money didn't matter to me just then. It should have, but it didn't. What mattered was putting out meaningful music in a meaningful way.

After that first collaboration with Bastille Records, Dim Mak was a one-man operation. I worked it on my own all the way to 2003, when I hired my first employee. Somewhere in there, early on, I put out a This Machine Kills EP, and then I put out a record for this other band I was playing in called The Fire Next Time. (I pinched the name of the band from a James Baldwin book I loved.) Each time out, I made enough money to make another record. That's all it was about for me—feeding the machine, seeding the community. Putting this music out into the world and hopefully shining a little bit of light on some of these up-and-coming artists.

Now that I had my own label, I was constantly on the prowl for new bands, always on the lookout for the next big thing. It's the same with my work now as a DJ. I'm not just out there looking for the new trends; I'm trying to get ahead of the trend. But you have to hit it just right. If you're too far out there, you're not going to find an audience. If you're lagging a little bit, then you're tired, dated, behind the curve. You have to be just *a little* ahead of the trend, so you can spot what's coming and shine just the right amount of light on it, at just the right time.

It's the Three Bears theory of being out there on the cutting edge. You don't want what you're putting out to be too cold. You don't want it to be too hot. You want it to be just right.

My favorite thing, in the early days of Dim Mak, was going to all these pressing plants to have the records made. The big thing back then was doing vinyl in all these different colors. You could even press the records into different geometric shapes—squares, triangles, whatever. This magical detail came into play when I was going through my files in preparation for this book. I wanted to dig out that very first Dim Mak release, just to hold it in my hands, to read my father's words on the endpiece, to remember the excitement Dan and the band felt when I told them I'd sold a bunch of copies at a hardcore show. It all came rushing back to me, like it happened just the other day, but what I'd completely forgotten was that we'd reached for the colored vinyl on that very first pressing. We split the run, actually—we did three hundred copies in traditional black vinyl and the other three hundred in . . . (wait for it!) . . . a fresh shade of baby blue, almost like a pastel.

Are you fucking kidding me? Dim Mak #1? On blue vinyl? See how it all ties in?

DROP

There is nothing quite so heartbreakingly blue as the bluebird sky that kisses Manhattan on the morning of September 11, 2001. I am in New York City on this day, so I should know, and yet I only know this from pictures, from footage, from written accounts.

I know from what I've been told.

I do not wake to the brilliant blue of that late summer sky, like so many millions of New Yorkers headed off to work. I do not start the day filled with hope, or the promise of something new. I do not turn my face to the sun and wonder at infinite possibility. No, I start the day in confusion, chaos. I am in my father's bedroom on the Upper East Side. He is out of town, opening a new Benihana location in Chicago with my brother Kevin, so I have slept in his bed. No biggie. Except everyone in my family is scrambling to find me. They know I am in town. They know I am supposed to be home. So once those planes hit and everyone in the city starts taking inventory of their friends and family, they cannot think where the hell I am, what the hell has happened to me.

It is my father's assistant, Toshi, who finally finds me. He comes into my father's room to look for something, and the noise wakes me up. He says, "Oh my goodness, Steven. You are here. We are looking for you."

It is ten o'clock in the morning, maybe eleven. I cannot think why anyone has been looking for me.

I am right here.

Toshi tells me about the attack, about the buildings coming down, about the terror and panic that have gripped the city. The world has gone from light to dark. His words make no sense to me. Sixteen years later, in Vegas, I will hear the news of another inexplicable terror in the same unimaginable way—unimaginable, as in, I have no way to imagine it. Toshi's words land like a ton of bricks, a blur, a non sequitur. I have no frame of reference for them. I race to the window and look outside, but the view does nothing to fill in the blanks of what Toshi is saying. It is just a brownstone, so all I see are other buildings . . . and the street below, and everything looks like it always looks.

I am so fucking confused. Scared. Outside of myself.

I think maybe someone is playing a cruel, sick joke, but just to be sure I tell myself I need to talk to my sister Devon. I remember being super-pissed at Devon the night before because she had an extra ticket to the Jackson Five concert at Madison Square Garden and decided to take our sister Echo instead of me. My anger seems so petty to me now, so small, up against what Toshi says has just happened at the World Trade Center. It is just last night, but it is a lifetime ago.

Devon answers her phone and tells me she is on a bus, headed out of the city. It is a tour bus belonging to the musician Lenny Kravitz, the guy she's been seeing. Devon is a big-time model, the face of Versace, and she moves around the city like she can do what she wants. She is a force of nature. She is my baby sister, but she is also my friend. We are close—so close she should have probably taken me to see the Jackson Five—but I do not dwell on this. I am pissed and not pissed. I am over it and I am not. I am so damn glad she is okay and out of the city.

Devon asks where I've been, and I tell her I've been asleep. "I'm in Dad's room," I say. "I'm just waking up."

She tells me she and Lenny could see the Twin Towers from their apartment, the smoke billowing from those buildings. She tells me she has never been more afraid. "You have to get out of the city, Steven," she says. "It's not safe."

I have a different reaction. My instinct is to head downtown, toward the World Trade Center. I am like an idiot climbing up a down escalator, a salmon swimming upstream. Everyone is moving in the opposite direction, but I am determined to push against the current. When I get as far as 20th Street, I start to run, toward the devastation. The whole time I am running, I do not look up . . . not once. I do not notice the brilliant blue sky until later, looking at images. I can only see the ash and smoke and soot, the desperate, anguished faces of the people scrambling uptown.

I can only see what is right in front of me.

At some point I start to cough. Like, a lot. It is difficult to breathe. The air is heavy, toxic. I pull the collar of my shirt to my nose and breathe through the fabric. This helps, but only a little. Only for a moment.

There is something pulling me downtown. I cannot say what it is. I cannot say why it is. It only is.

I am walking, walking, walking. Looking dead ahead. Struggling to breathe. Seeing but not really seeing the agony in the onrush of people coming toward me. It is like nothing in my experience. I walk as far as I can, until a line of police tape blocks my path. The whole time, I am working my flip phone, trying to locate my few friends in town. Devon has told me that everyone in my family is safe, so I worry about my friends, but the airwaves are crowded with millions of people trying to place their own frantic, worried calls, so I cannot get through.

Somehow, a call comes through to me—one of my friends, doing his version of the same thing. He tells me where he is and I make my way to him—still against the current, but in a different direction. A group of us meet in Union Square. We hug. We cry. We compare stories. I notice one of my friends has a camcorder—a long-lens Canon GL2. I ask if I can borrow it, sling it around my neck, head back out to see what I can see.

I do this without thinking.

I start to grab people on the street and ask them to talk to me. I point the camera in their direction and push them to tell me what they have seen, where they were when the buildings fell, where they are going. I talk to cabbies stuck in gridlock traffic, through the open windows of their cars.

For two days, I talk to people in this way. Never face-to-face. Always through the camera. It is as if there is no longer any room on this planet for normal human interaction, and I need to place some artifice between me and everyone else. I can hide behind the lens of this Canon GL2 and pretend that this horror show of a nightmare is happening in some other city, to some other group of people.

We are, all of us, once removed.

I do not know what I expect to find through these interviews. I do not know what I am looking for. But I am driven by the work. New York City is impenetrable, unrecognizable. You cannot get on or off the island of Manhattan, not easily. The bridges and tunnels are on lockdown. Our minds are on lockdown. And so I tiptoe through the streets, peering in at people's souls through the long lens of my friend's Canon GL2.

Together with another UC Santa Barbara friend, I decide to compile these interviews into a documentary. We will call it Carpet of Gold, Carpet of Bombs. I do not *know how we come up with this title, but it speaks to us in some way.*

I am not a DJ yet, but I suppose I am a DJ in my bones. Already, I am trying to find music in the face of madness, to create art from the insights of others. I do not have the words to express myself, so I am tapping the souls of these wretched strangers, hoping they might give voice to what I cannot imagine.

Together, my friend and I will conduct dozens of interviews. We will apply for a grant. We will speak to Howard Zinn, rest in peace, the noted historian. We will travel to interview Noam Chomsky, Alice Walker . . . We want to hear from cabbies and activists and citizen-soldiers and agents of change. We want to hear from people who were in those buildings, from people who lost people who were in those buildings.

We will assemble hours and hours of recordings, but I will never look at them. My friend and partner will never look at them. The project will be abandoned. I tell myself that because it was never fully realized it can never be completed.

It is a place to put our sadness, is all.

And, surely, it is a place to store the frighteningly blue sky of that long-ago September morning. A sky I never really saw for myself, straight on, and could only capture on videotape as I pointed my friend's camcorder this way and that.

7

LICK THE PAVEMENT CLEAN

Wasn't planning on becoming a DJ. Never even thought about it. And so the story of how I went from an aspiring musician to a promoter to a record label "executive" to where I am now is a lesson in resilience, resourcefulness.

Also, dumb luck.

Thing is, I wasn't much of a businessman early on. I was good at spotting talent, nurturing talent, promoting talent, but that's about where my skill set ran thin. Yeah, I was making noise at Dim Mak, getting my groove on in Los Angeles, but I wasn't making money. In fact, I was losing money—like, a shit-ton. My strengths and my weaknesses were kind of canceling each other out, so I was mostly treading water.

But I kept at it, because I was a fan at heart and I was having a blast, and Dim Mak gave me a front-row seat to the bands I loved, the music I loved. Best example of this was my work with The Kills. I had a US distribution deal with them. They had a separate deal in the UK, but I was their guy in the States—and, if you remember, for a hot while they were probably the most talked-about underground indie band on the scene. Their sound had this immersive Chrissie Hynde vibe, but it was also edgy and bluesy. It had a feel to it that was familiar and at the same time brand fucking new, and I was just a passionate, passionate fan—so completely honored that they trusted me to champion what they were doing. I went on the road with them, became their tour manager, hustled my tail off, did whatever you do when you're jump-starting a career—theirs, mine, whatever. Plus, these guys were my friends. Alison Mosshart and Jamie Hince. They treated me like a member of the band. A lot of times, it was just the three of us, tooling around in a little van. I would drive, or Jamie would drive, or Alison would drive. We would listen to Captain Beefheart on the road. We must've listened to those *Trout Mask Replica* and *Safe as Milk* albums forty or fifty times, all the way through. Everything they listened to, I digested. What they were into, I was into. I sold their merch, struggled to wake them up for lobby calls, talked them through whatever shit they were dealing with. I would have taken a bullet for these guys, I loved them so much.

To be fair, I was a shit tour manager, and I wasn't set up at Dim Mak to fully service Alison and Jamie once they started to happen in a big-time way. Like a lot of the bands I was promoting, The Kills got to this place where they were ready to graduate from Dim Mak and take the next step up the ladder. I understood that progression—I didn't love it, but I understood it.

I remember going in to talk to Keith Wood, who was the main guy at Rough Trade Records in the US office, and we were going over all these receipts from The Kills' tour, and it was clear to both of us that I had no idea what I was doing. I was just a kid. I didn't know what it meant to stick to a budget, and after a while Keith just looked up at me and said, "Dude, we need you off the road. You suck at this."

He was right. But what I didn't suck at was finding these acts ahead of the major labels, and propping them up in my own DIY, indie way.

It went to my head, the success I was having with a lot of my Dim Mak artists. Soon, all these major labels wanted to talk to me about maybe seeding their talent roster, incubating some of these up-and-coming bands, helping them to spot the next big thing. I loved that all these A&R guys were starting to hit me up. I loved that they thought I had something to offer. All that talk filled my head. All the noise my bands were making . . . that filled my head, too. I started thinking I was the shit, started turning down some tremendous opportunities, just because it felt to me like I wasn't being treated with the respect I arrogantly thought I deserved. Like when Arcade Fire was about to pop. Their manager when they were coming up was also their lawyer, and she reached out to me, said she had the most incredible band from Montreal, sent me their *Funeral* album, which had just been completed. The album was absolutely stunning—I was blown away. So I called her back and said I wanted Dim Mak to do the album, but she wasn't offering me the album. The album had already been signed away. What she was offering was an EP, which the band was calling "No Cars Go."

I said, "If you don't give me the album, I don't want it." Like an idiot.

To this day, I kick myself that I let Arcade Fire get away from Dim Mak just because of my ego. Just because my reach had started to exceed my grasp and I was starting to get a little too full of myself. Keep in mind, Arcade Fire probably had no idea this woman was reaching out, because these were early, early days for the band. They didn't have a big team behind them. They were all scrambling, and this lawyer/manager was just trying to get their demo out ahead of the album, maybe get a buzz going, thinking we could help each other out.

And we could have, if my head had been a little smaller, and here it would be good to report that I learned my lesson after this one misstep and immediately set things right, but that's not exactly how it went down. There's a learning curve, you know. You figure it out as you go along. You get taken down a couple pegs and you start to realize you're not all that . . . you're only a *little bit* of that.

Meanwhile, I was hitting the Los Angeles music scene—smacking the shit out of it, actually. I was out every night, bouncing from one club to the next, always on the lookout for the next big thing. I'd work all day on Dim Mak stuff and go out all night—not exactly the best mix for a healthy lifestyle, but I was young and invincible and feeling like I was on top of the world.

There was this bar I used to go to in those days called Three Clubs, on the corner of Santa Monica and Vine. I was living in central Hollywood, in a crappy-great apartment: nine hundred square feet, nine hundred bucks. A good deal, if you didn't mind the neighborhood, which felt like the epicenter for every drug dealer, pimp, and prostitute in town. My street was beyond sketchy, but I loved it. There was a ton of excitement, this sense that anything could happen, at any time, and I was right in the middle of it.

There was a bartender at Three Clubs named Cali DeWitt, and he became my very first true friend in Los Angeles. Turned out he knew who I was, knew about Dim Mak, had been to a couple Pickle Patch shows in Santa Barbara . . . had even been to see some of the bands I used to play with. We were cut in a lot of the same ways. Cali was a punk kid at heart, with long-standing roots in the local music scene. His brother Nick was the drummer for a band I'd signed to Dim Mak called Pretty Girls Make Graves—a name they'd pinched from a line in Jack Kerouac's *The Dharma Bums*.

We hit it off. Cali had this insane record collection, and he thought my collection was solid, so we were always talking about records, listening to records, going to see all these new bands. We were part of a very small subset of the culture that was big into vinyl, big into learning everything there was to know about our favorite artists. It was like an obsession with us.

One night, he put it out that he wanted me to DJ at his bar—said he thought it'd be cool for me to bring some of my records down, maybe turn people on to some of the music and artists we loved. He said, "Your collection is sick. People will be into it."

I didn't even understand what it meant to DJ, to work with two turntables and a mixer. But Cali said he had whatever equipment I'd need, and that he'd show me how to do it.

His idea was to run a special promo night called Sides, where people like me would come in and play entire sides of our favorite records—presumably in front of a bar filled with a whole bunch of *other* people like me.

He said, "Play whatever you want."

I said, "Hardcore?"

He said, "Whatever."

Cali couldn't pay me, other than letting me run a bar tab—probably didn't even occur to me that I should be paid. Wasn't any kind of career move. It was just me spinning records at a small corner bar, for maybe forty, fifty people. But I showed up at Three Clubs with a couple crates of records—seven-inch, twelve-inch. They weren't dance records. They weren't hip-hop records. I had no idea if the people at the bar would be into my music, but Cali said to play what I wanted, so I took him at his word. He sat me down in the back corner, showed me how to use the two turntables he had set up—straightforward stuff, you know. He showed me what the needles were designed to do, how to use the mixer. I had a record player at home, and I'd logged some time at our college radio station, so I wasn't flying completely blind. I was a long way from beat-matching, but I had the basics down. I might not have been ready to *really* call myself a DJ, but I could put together the most lit Spotify-type playlist and fill the room with the music that mattered to me.

As long as I'm coming completely clean on my rookie abilities as a DJ, I guess I should clarify my role at my college radio station. I never got a chance to do my thing at the main campus radio station, KCSB, but I did have an overnight slot at our second-tier station, KJUC, which we all called K-Juice. The name was a bit of an overstatement, because there wasn't a whole lot of juice to what we were doing. We were a minor-league operation, and you could only pick up our signal in this one little corner of campus. I was convinced I was broadcasting into a vacuum, and there were a lot of nights when I'd challenge listeners to call in with a request, or just to let me know they were out there. I'd threaten to play Extreme's "More Than Words" on a back-to-back loop if I didn't get a call in the next ten minutes, or whatever, and that usually did the trick.

Back to my DJ debut . . .

The very first song I dropped that night at Three Clubs was a cut off Born Against's *Nine Patriotic Hymns for Children*, and in keeping with the theme of this book I'm happy to report that the album jacket was an image of an American flag set against a blue background.

(It's *all* blue!)

When the music came on, I looked out across the bar and saw this sea of confused, annoyed faces. Don't know what kind of music those folks were into, but it sure as hell wasn't . . . *this*. But Cali was digging it, and I guess he was the guy I was playing to. He didn't give a fuck—and, just then, neither did I. All I cared about was playing my records, letting my music *breathe*. It felt to me like a kind of calling, like it was on me to spin this music and put it out in the world. (It would be a while before I figured out that the job of DJs is to help people have a good time, not to amuse themselves by cranking the volume on their cherished records. To play what people wanted to hear.) Cali's deal was to disrupt, shake things up, push people's buttons—and bringing me in to share my hardcore collection was just one way to do that. He'd go on to design clothes for Kanye West, and to become a true visionary in the LA street-culture scene, but here he was just mixing drinks and kicking up a little dust.

Out of that first gig, Cali and I decided to form our own DJ group. Wasn't like my debut as a DJ was any kind of runaway success, but we were caught up in it. We would just play hardcore punk records. We would call ourselves DJ Cry Babies. I would be DJ Cry, and Cali would be DJ Babies—only we never actually got around to playing anywhere. We just talked about it, same way we used to talk about all the things we wanted to do in and around the local music scene. And it just worked out that this was the one and only time I DJed at Three Clubs—not because I sucked at it so much but because it just never came up again. Cali would get these wild ideas all the time, his head was always spinning, and by the end of the week his Sides idea was played.

I kept going out to all these bars, all these clubs, and now that I was in the mix I was looking for places to play my music. I got it in my head that it was like spinning records at K-Juice, only here there'd be a bunch of people right in front of me, so I could play to an audience. That Three Clubs scene wasn't really *my* scene; I was hoping to play for some like-minded souls. I'd spent all those years putting together this massive record collection, and now my buddy Cali had turned me on to the idea of maybe sharing it, so I wanted to keep that going. I liked the idea of turning people on to a whole new sound, or maybe reintroducing them to a style of music they hadn't heard in a while.

There was this one club I went to, Echo, and I eventually talked my way into a DJ gig there. By this point, I think I'd played a half-dozen or so sets around town and I still didn't have any equipment of my own. I didn't even have a name, was just going by Steve Aoki, although there was a time or two in there when I billed myself as DJ Cry—just, you know, to try it out.

I was spending a lot of time at Amoeba Music, this record shop I used to go to, buying up all kinds of records. I was starting to realize that I needed to play a little bit of everything, so I loaded up on hip-hop, house, R&B, indie, dance music . . . whatever I thought would get a crowd moving. Not only was I not getting paid for these gigs—I was shelling out money to fill in some of the holes in my collection.

When the gig came around on the calendar, I showed up at Echo with all these new records and set up to do my thing. There was an emcee on the mic trying to hype up the crowd. I had this Kelis song cued up I was going to open with called "Millionaire," featuring André 3000, and the emcee came over to me to ask how I wanted to be billed. It just worked out that there was this line from the song that went, "Mama, I'm a millionaire," and it was stuck in my head, so I said, "Hey, I'm Mama Millionaire."

The emcee looked at me like I was brainless—said, "Yo, that's no dude's name. You can't be Mama Millionaire. You should be Papa Billionaire."

I didn't like the sound of that one, so I gave it some thought—not a lot, but some, 'cause I was about to go on. I couldn't be "Papa" anything, I was just a kid, and from there I made the leap to thinking I could be Kid Millionaire, so I put it out there.

The emcee went out to introduce me—"Put your hands together for DJ Kid Millionaire!"—and it rang like bells in a church. I thought, *Holy shit! Great fucking name!*

And it was. For a while.

So I started going by DJ Kid Millionaire, and it stuck. A couple weeks later, the name had grown big enough to get me my first paying gig, at another club I used to go to called Spaceland, and here again my head for business didn't do me any favors. The gig paid $75, but for the first time I had to bring my own sound system, so I hit up my friends, friends of friends. Nobody had the right mix of speakers and turntables, so I had to scramble. (Shout-out to my friend Sam Spiegel for hooking me up with whatever I needed!) It ended up that I had to lay out about $100 just to "borrow" all this equipment and get it set up, and it didn't take a genius to see the math didn't exactly make sense.

Still, I did the gig and counted it a good deal. I mean, it was a *paying* gig, right? That's the way my mind worked—or, the way it *didn't* work, I guess. I told myself it was a step up from the shows I'd been doing for free, even though it was actually costing me money and I was coming out behind.

It would have helped if I didn't suck. I was spinning my own vinyl, learning on the fly, and it just wasn't happening. I was train-wrecking, big-time, but I got better as the night went along. Each time out, I'd discover something new—some new technique or trick of the trade—and here on this first paying gig I finally had my song selection down. I was playing to the crowd. Notorious B.I.G. Bloc Party. LCD Soundsystem. Wasn't exactly *my* music, but people were up, moving, having a big old time.

End of the night, I went up to the guy who ran the place and asked if I could maybe play there again.

He said, "Guess so."

(Not exactly a ringing endorsement—but I'd take whatever I could get.)

I said, "One thing, though. It cost me a hundred bucks to rent all this gear. Any chance you could give me another twenty-five dollars so I'm not out of pocket?"

And here it's not like the guy even had to think about it. He just said, "Actually, no. Was thinking of giving you fifty next time, because you weren't very good."

So that was my last paying gig for a while.

Cut to a couple months later, when I ran into a friend of mine named Frankie Chan, outside this venue called El Rey. He was passing out flyers for a Thursday-night party he was throwing called Fucking Awesome. Frankie had this whole fun, indie thing happening with that party; I'd been by a few times, and we got to talking. I told him about the DJ gigs I was trying to line up, and he already knew me as a promoter. He knew what I had going on with Dim Mak, knew I was plugged-in around town, knew I had this rep as an indie record guy with all these cool underground connections.

Frankie and Har Mar Superstar were the main DJs of the party, and they were buddies with two guys named Mike Piscitelli and Jason Dill, who had this very small streetwear brand called "Fucking Awesome," and that's where they got the name. The brand was so small they would literally just make shirts for their friends, but it had a whole lot of cred, even in this small way.

Whatever Frankie had going on with his Fucking Awesome party, I wanted in, so I asked if he needed any help handing out flyers, hustling, getting the word out. Told him I just wanted to help him fill the room and play a set. Don't know why, but I was really selling myself, wanting to get some traction going on the DJ front, and Frankie was willing to give me a shot. Maybe it's because that party reminded me in some way of the Pickle Patch shows we used to stage in Santa Barbara. It was homemade, homespun, bare-bones. It was authentic. I wasn't thinking in any kind of scheming way—like how great it would be to have a venue to break our Dim Mak artists. No, it was more of a sideline pursuit, something to do to fill the time, maybe rediscover the stoke that lit me and my housemates back in college, when we were putting on all those shows—and yeah, maybe there'd be some crossover benefit to what we were trying to build over at Dim Mak, but that would have just been a bonus at this point.

Frankie told me I could play, but I would have to play for free. After that, if everything worked out, he'd be able to pay me fifty bucks a throw.

Sounded good to me. I mean, I'd get my name on the flyer. I'd be on the bill with Har Mar Superstar, the main DJ who was headlining the party. It wasn't much, but at the same time, it was a big, big deal . . . it was *fucking awesome!*

That first night, I was the opening DJ. I was playing as people were filing in, which meant I was just playing to the bartenders. There was a lot of chatter, wasn't exactly an ideal setup, but I was determined to make it work. I had my crates of records, I had an idea in my mind of the music I would play, but then of course you've got to read the mood of the room, get a feel for the moment, change things up. And I figured it out, to where Frankie asked me back, to where Frankie started paying me, to where I began to develop my own little following . . . even to where we became partners.

Here again, I want to stress that the Fucking Awesome party wasn't my deal. It had been going on before I got there. I didn't start it . . . I didn't name it . . . but once I signed on I kind of helped it along. The party was held in a small, retro-type bar in Hollywood called the Beauty Bar, done up to look like an old-fashioned beauty salon. There were salon-style chairs and hair dryers lined up on one side of the wall to make the place look like a throwback to the beauty parlors of the fifties and sixties. It had a kitschy feel that people seemed to dig—only you couldn't fit too many people in there comfortably. Uncomfortably, we could probably squeeze in 100, 125 people. The place was maybe a couple hundred square feet, with a bar on one side of the room, the DJ booth tucked all the way in the back. You couldn't even see the booth, really—all night long, people would stumble upon it and think maybe it was the coat check room.

Still, I was lucky to be there, happy for the opportunity, even if it was a shit gig starting out. First couple times, I actually got there way early, so I could get comfortable working the turntables. The bartenders would be laughing as they were setting up because I was just so awful. I got better at it, though, but it's not like there was this intense pressure to step up my game—people weren't coming out to the Beauty Bar to hear the opening DJ anyway. Matter of fact, that was pretty much the culture at the time, all over town. If you weren't a top-tier celebrity DJ, nobody really gave a shit about you or your set. That explained the nothing-special DJ booth we had in the back, where no one could really see you, but the thing about downplaying your DJ booth like that is that it's hard to get a party going. The energy is where the DJ is, right? So it follows that if you put the DJ in the corner, there's no energy.

That all started to change with our Fucking Awesome party. The room quickly filled with energy . . . kinetic, frenetic, combustible energy. Thursday nights, we were the place to be. All these great indie-hipster bands coming through town would make it a point to check us out. We set it up so we were like the after-party following their shows. In our own little world, we were blowing up, turning people away at the door. Every week, we were slammed, and the noise we were making just got louder and louder.

The whole time, I was still finding my way as a DJ. If anything, I was more of a curator than a true DJ back then. A trend-spotter, a tastemaker. I had the music part down, but I was still finding my way on the technical side. My thing was to share the bands I loved in this underground way. No pretense. No staging. No bells and whistles. It was just a way to keep the party going, to promote our Dim Mak artists, earn a little extra money on the side.

Eventually, the main DJ started going out on tour and it fell to me to headline, and that gave us the legs to do more parties. Within a couple months, our Fucking Awesome parties started to morph into the Dim Mak Tuesdays parties I ended up running for a bunch of years in a bigger venue up the street—an old movie theater called Cinespace. That party just exploded, became the most poppin' indie party in LA. We had all the big-time bands coming to DJ: Interpol, the Shins, the Killers, the Yeah Yeah Yeahs . . .

If you step back and trace the genealogy of it, our Cinespace hookup came straight out of our Beauty Bar parties. That's how it usually worked in our underground culture—one thing led to another. How it worked here was we'd struck up a friendship with a guy named Jason Stewart—an artist/promoter who went by the name Them Jeans. Jason was this freakishly tall fixture on the scene, maybe 6'10", so he really stood out. Hard not to notice. He was coming to all of our parties, and he took us aside one night and told us he had an open slot at this old movie theater that had been converted into an event space. The place was huge compared to our Beauty Bar digs. It was originally a kind of dinner-and-a-movie lounge, so there was a lot of unconventional space. There was a small room in front, maybe four hundred square feet, but then there was this giant open space, with room for maybe six hundred people. And, a stage! So—fuck, yeah!—we jumped at the chance to move our party over there.

Things kicked up a whole bunch of notches with this move to Cinespace, which was where all these cultures started to collide. By this point, I'd been DJing at parties for all these different magazines—five, six, seven parties a week—and now we had a stage where some of these artists who had been coming through for our parties could actually perform. Rock acts, pop acts, hip-hop acts, other DJs . . . we were already out there on that cutting edge, but now these artists had a place to play. One of the great side benefits to these parties, that "bonus" I talked about earlier, was the way these gigs let me feature a lot of our Dim Mak artists. They gave us an important platform, but off that we started showcasing all these other up-and-coming acts as well. Labels were hitting us up, managers and agents, everybody wanting to get their talent in on our scene, and we put it out there that there was room enough under our tent for everyone. And just like it was with the Pickle Patch phenomenon we'd created back in Santa Barbara, people started to think that you weren't happening as an artist in town if you weren't happening under our roof.

One thing about our Cinespace setup: almost as soon as we started doing our thing there, we moved our DJ booth front and center, and it just worked out that the best spot for it was up against a brick wall. Trouble was, we blasted the music so loud in there, I ended up with permanent damage to my left ear—an occupational hazard, I guess. The trade-off, though, was that the DJ began to take on a more prominent role. Wasn't just me, in that spot. It was like a shift in the culture.

Our personalities were out there.

Our energy was out there.

We were out there.

After a while, I became a partner in the venue, and our Cinespace

Tuesdays became Dim Mak Tuesdays—a never-ending party that ran for over ten years. It was around this time I started working with my manager, Matt Colon. That gets a shout here for how it came about, because it was an unlikely collaboration. Matt was working as the marketing director for *BPM* and *Vapors*, two influential magazines on the dance and indie-hipster scenes. The sister publications used to host a monthly party at Cinespace on Tuesdays, until our Tuesday party started to blow up and they had to move to another night. Over the next year or so, we developed a good working friendship. Things could have gone another way between us, I guess, because we'd kind of pushed the magazines off their spot on the calendar, but Matt wasn't like that. We got along. He would bring me on to DJ at a lot of his parties—in San Francisco, New York, and Miami, as well as Los Angeles—because I was a good reflection of that hipster, skateboarder vibe he had going with *Vapors*. In those days, I was known more as a promoter and an indie-label guy than a DJ, so I didn't really belong in the pages of *BPM* just yet, or at their parties. But with *Vapors*, I fit right in.

After a while, Matt's parties became a bigger deal than the magazines they were meant to promote. The business kind of flipped away from print and into this event culture that was taking shape. Matt and I used to travel together during this time, and we'd hang out a lot when we were in LA. I can remember a conversation we had one night over dinner at a Thai restaurant on Hollywood Boulevard, where I was whining about how difficult it was for me to track all the booking requests that were starting to come my way. I'd never been great about responding to the pile of emails lining up in my in-box, so I was missing out on gigs that would come and go before I could even respond to an invitation for me to DJ. Yeah, those gigs were only paying me $100 or so, maybe $200, but I was counting on that extra money to cover my bills.

I said, "I need someone to keep me on track with all of this."

Matt said, "I'll do it for you."

And that's how our partnership was born. We started with a handshake. It took a couple years for Matt to sign on full-time. He kept doing his thing for the magazines, but after a while there was enough money coming in for him to step away from his day job. One of his first acts on my behalf was to convince me to reject all those $100 and $200 offers that came my way. He put it out there that I wouldn't show up for less than $500, and I remember being a little freaked out about that, thinking nobody would pay me that kind of money, but the offers kept coming in at about the same rate. I was grateful to Matt for pushing me to rethink what I was worth.

One of the first big gigs he set up for me was a Super Bowl after-party in Detroit, early on in 2006. The party was being thrown by Hewlett-Packard, and somehow Matt was able to get me $5,000 for an appearance. The number was astronomical—*way* more than I'd ever seen on one deal. It was a good payday for Matt, too, with his 10 percent cut, so we set off for Detroit feeling pretty great about ourselves. I'd be playing with Queens of the Stone Age, who were just out with their *Lullabies to Paralyze* album, so this was a huge deal—but we almost missed the party. We fell asleep at the gate, and we didn't hear the damn boarding call for our connecting flight, even though we were sitting in the first row of chairs in the waiting area. They kept calling our names, and calling our names, and we were there the whole fucking time, and when we finally woke up we had to scramble to get our asses on another plane. In the end, Matt had to call ahead and arrange for a police escort to get us to the event through all that Super Bowl traffic, but we managed to make it there with a couple minutes to spare.

It was around this time, too, that I first met Adam Goldstein—DJ AM—who started coming to our parties in 2005 or so. I'll write more about AM a little later on in these pages, but for now I just want to put it out there that he was the great exception to my nobody-gives-a-shit-about-DJs observation. He was the king of the DJs. He was the one dating Nicole Richie, the one playing private parties for celebrity clients like Tom Cruise and Leonardo DiCaprio, the one with the household name. The rest of us were just pretenders to his throne, so when he started coming to our parties to check us out, I was floored. Oh, man . . . there's no way to overstate the influence this guy was having on our emerging scene, so just having him at one of our parties was major. Having him become a *regular* . . . are you fucking kidding me?

You have to remember, this was back before social media. These were the days of MySpace and Instant Messaging, which essentially meant you had to actually *be* in the clubs to find out about this music. You had to *be* in the scene to experience the scene. You couldn't do it in your bedroom, you had to get off your ass and seek it out, and like any good curator/tastemaker/promoter, DJ AM was out there checking it out. Checking *us* out.

Out of *that*, we decided to put our heads together and launch a whole new party—Banana Split, which was like the culmination of everything we'd been doing in our separate orbits. It was this great convergence of underground culture and mainstream culture . . . and after that it was only a matter of time before some of AM's huge star power started to rub off on little old me.

I look back on that time and I still get chills. We had all these amazing artists coming through. will.i.am. The Black Eyed Peas. LMFAO. Skrillex. Kanye West. Our parties became a *thing*, and DJs from around the world came to soak up the culture, to taste what we were putting out there. It was a magical, meaningful time—a tsunami of music and art and a moment that hasn't really been duplicated since. I was so fucking thrilled to be in its middle—God, it was insane. Los Angeles was like this great magnet for all these tremendous artists—still is!—so eventually we had all these groundbreaking talents turn up to play: Lady Gaga, Kid Cudi, M.I.A. . . . Really, it makes my head spin, just to think of the artists we were able to feature. If you were an artist coming up, if you were a producer, a head of a label, you had to come out to our parties. From Jimmy Iovine to the Killers to Drake . . . it felt to us like we *were* the music scene.

I'm not putting this out there to blow smoke—this was how it was.

One thing I hadn't counted on, though, was how my DJ name might get me into some trouble, once people actually knew who I was. I should have seen it coming. I'd just liked the sound of it, you know. DJ Kid Millionaire. Never really thought it all the way through, but then, when the DJ thing really started to percolate, when the editors of

BPM magazine finally decided to put me on the cover, I caught a lot of heat for it. The editors of the magazine took a lot of heat for it, too, mostly because I'd yet to earn my cred as a DJ. The haters lined up against me, started talking shit about how the "Son of Benihana" had his chest out, was boasting about having all that money. Wasn't like that, though. Wasn't like my father had given any of us a thing, other than his name and his work ethic. All those years, me scrambling to make my rent, me digging my way out from under the pile of debt I was racking up at Dim Mak, me spending $200 on a plane ticket to fly to a $100 DJ gig, me pinching copies from Kinko's to promote my shows while my buddy Mike Phyte looked the other way . . . I was DIY, all the way. Self-made, all the way. Figuring it out, in what ways I could. Holding all these moving parts together with grit and Scotch tape.

The criticism stung. I'd spent my whole life getting teased and taunted for who I was, for who I wasn't. I could never quite fit myself in, growing up in Newport Beach. I bounced around to all these different schools. I was the quintessential outsider, and it didn't help that I had a father who seemed to thrive when he was out of his element. Mostly, it didn't help that I had a father who was mentioned in the newspaper. The other kids would jump to all these conclusions about me, thinking that because my father ran this famous chain of restaurants, that meant I was rich, or thought I was special, or entitled. Wasn't like that, either. But try telling that to a bunch of middle-school kids who were just scrambling to fit in themselves.

So when I started getting all this negative feedback on my DJ name, I tried to transition from it right away. Couldn't shed DJ Kid Millionaire entirely—I had to phase it out over the next while, because that was how I'd become known. I started booking myself as "Steve Aoki, Kid Millionaire," and then eventually I was able to drop the stage name and just do my thing as myself.

Wherever this DJ thing was gonna take me, it would take me as I was.

DROP

It is World Autism Awareness Day.

The White House is blue.

The Empire State Building is blue.

The Eiffel Tower is blue.

Skylines, bridges, landmarks all over the world . . . blue. The fucking Sphinx and the Great Pyramids of Egypt and Niagara Falls and all the great wonders of the world are bathed in deep blue light.

My social media feeds are bursting with blue.

And so I wonder: What is it about the color blue that attaches to a diagnosis of autism in this way? Yeah, I know from the researchers I've tapped who study the human brain that certain colors can affect our mood states. I get that blue can be a calming trigger—it tells us all is right in our world. But what I don't get is the symbolism that shines a blue light on what it means to live with autism. It's completely new to me, and as I take in all these images, I wonder how this is something I've missed. The study of the human brain has become my abiding passion, away from music. I want to know how it works, how it doesn't. I've put together this great network of top scientists, who very patiently walk me through all these breakthrough discoveries and turn me on to what it all might mean, so I reach out on this. I ask around, and nobody seems to know what the color blue signifies when it comes to autism. I look online, and nobody seems to know.

Best I can tell, the international symbol for autism is that familiar multicolored puzzle piece. It's blue, red, green, and yellow. You've probably seen it on T-shirts, hats, banners, whatever. The colors are meant to represent all the colors on the spectrum, reminding us that whether or not we carry a diagnosis of autism spectrum disorder, we all sit somewhere on that spectrum. The human palette is filled with countless shades. The puzzle piece is meant to represent the ways we all fit together. Whatever our reality is, whatever our perception is, whatever our abilities are, they link up in some way to the realities, perceptions, abilities we all share.

That's such a powerful message, when you break it down. Such a powerful image. It puts it out there that we are made whole by the ways we adjust to each other, the ways we compensate for each other. One person's suffering is absorbed by another's abundance. One family's hardship is made easier by another family's generosity. The idea is we can accommodate, adjust to anything, long as we work as a cohesive unit. Long as our big picture is clear.

At least that's how I see it. People bring their own meaning to the symbol, I guess—to the colors, too. But what strikes me today is how we're meant to "light it up blue" to promote autism awareness. Why blue? What happened to those other colors? There's some controversy to this, I'm learning. A lot of folks say the focus on blue comes from a marketing effort by Autism Speaks, probably the most influential advocacy group dedicated to individuals and families on the spectrum. Turns out this global awareness day is pretty much their deal, and this is what the brand has become. In fact, some municipalities won't light their buildings or their public spaces blue because they see it as some kind of *fund-raiser. For years, the White House wouldn't participate. Governments around the world wouldn't participate.*

And now they do—so, end of the day, who cares what's behind this initiative? It's struck a chord, and that chord is resonating, and that chord is blue. The message is going viral, and it's lit by the deep blue of hope and acceptance, and as we stop to reach for that blue T-shirt in the back of our dresser drawer, or the blue lightbulb we used to light our front walkway at some years-ago party, we're finding ways to connect with each other, to support each other, to accommodate each other . . . and in this way the color can knit us together.

We are all the same, in the end. We are all on the same spectrum. We are blue with compassion for the suffering of these families. We are blue with admiration, at the strength they find a way to tap every day. We are blue with joy, at the blessings we breathe into the lives of the people who care for us.

8

WOULDN'T BE ME WITHOUT U

I n a lot of ways—in fact, in almost *every* way—I was never as close to my father as I was when he was dying.

There is something intimate about death when you see it coming. Something healing. It can rip you to pieces as it makes you whole.

The curious thing about my father's death was the way it brought us all together. The many branches of the family tree I wrote about earlier had scattered. We were all over the place, making our own music. For years, my father had been a kind of magnet, pulling us into his world, and now here he was, in the summer of 2008, drawing us in once more.

I refused to accept that my father was dying. We all did, I think. To his children, he was this larger-than-life figure: heroic, invincible, electric. He was a survivor, most of all. I don't think any one of us could have imagined a world without him in it, even as he stood in silent authority over the choices we were making in our dovetailing worlds, the lives we were living, alone and together.

His approval meant the world to me. And I was only just earning it. I was just a year or so removed from my first set at Coachella, starting to make a name for myself as a DJ—my name, *his* name. There was money coming in, at fucking last. Dim Mak was finally whole. Looking back, all these years later, I tend to race over the ways we struggled at the label. I don't do this to blow smoke or to bury the truth of how things were, but in my mind our successes counted above all. So, yeah, I'd shout about all the acts we were breaking, the impact we were making, the trends we were helping to shift and shape, and race over the fact that we were piling up debt. The one was lasting. The other was fleeting. We were in the red so damn long at Dim Mak, so damn deep, it almost didn't register when we were finally in the black. I kept telling myself that in the end it would all shake out to the good, and now that it was I wanted to tell my father about it. That was always a big driver for me, pushing myself to a place that would make him proud.

To this day, my dad almost ten years gone, whenever something good finds me in my career, I want to tell him about it. Whenever I push past some difficulty, I want to tell him about it. I wish more than anything that he could see how I live, what I've become. For my brothers and sisters, they might think about how they are as parents, in ways that relate to him. Some of them probably think about the legacies they're building through his grandchildren, but I'm not there just yet.

For me, for now, I want my father to see how my music brings people together, same way his restaurants brought people together. I want him to know that the choices I made, the choices he didn't always agree with, amounted to something.

I want him to taste the sweetness I have tasted, the sweetness my siblings have tasted.

I want him to know we're all okay.

I want him to see the ways I am just like him. I work hard, play hard. I live in the moment. I believe anything is possible.

But, hey, superheroes don't beat lung cancer, diabetes, hep C, cirrhosis of the liver, pneumonia. It took a couple months for all of that shit to finally slow my father down, and it sucked that just as he was slowing down I was ramping up, but we don't get to schedule these life-and-death battles. They hit you when they hit you, and when they hit my father we all dropped whatever we were doing and flew to be at his side. Me, I was in Ibiza, mostly. I'd started playing there the year before—a giant step for me. They didn't always roll out the welcome mat for American DJs in Ibiza, the global pulse of the dance music scene, but I was blessed to land a residency at a nightclub called Space. I was flying in every couple weeks for a weekend of shows, and when my father got sick it sometimes worked out that as soon as I touched down on the island I'd have to double back to the hospital in New York, without even playing a single set.

For months, things went on in this way. It'd look like my father was doing okay and that I could fly to Spain and do my shows, but then I'd get a call from my sister Grace, telling me to come back home.

Always, his kids filled the hospital room. Always, his third wife, Keiko, was a kind of supervising presence, deciding who would get to see him and when. She ran the show. It had been that way for a while, going back to before my father was sick. It used to be she kept me from the house, kept me from seeing my father, kept us from connecting. On the Benihana front, she kept us from the boardroom, from the kitchen, from the front of the house. It felt to me like the only way she could feel secure in her place by his side was to keep the rest of us from his side. But then, in the end, she knew she couldn't keep us from seeing him. I think she knew what it meant for us kids to have to face the thought of losing our father, what it meant for our father to have to face the thought of losing his kids. So she gave us our space, let us do our thing—only it sometimes felt to me like our grieving couldn't happen all at once.

There was one night, late, a bunch of us gathered in his hospital room, when Keiko stood abruptly and announced she had to leave to walk her dog Mugi. It took us all by surprise, her standing to leave like that, just then. My father most of all. He wasn't speaking then, had this little notepad he kept by his bed, and he reached for it. We all stood as he scratched out a message to Keiko: "Don't go."

For whatever reason, Keiko had it in her head that she needed to step out for a beat—said, "Your children are here. I need to walk the dog."

He grabbed the pad again—scrawled, "Stay."

But she was gone.

We all deal with our sadness in our own way, I guess, and maybe

Keiko's way was to just step away, you know. Or maybe she was giving us all some space, taking her own time to breathe. It was something to notice, that's all. But she was my father's wife. He'd chosen her. He knew who she was, and he'd chosen her. And she was free to grieve in her own way, on her own time.

In the very last conversation I had with my father, he told me he wasn't going to die. He didn't say he wasn't prepared to die, didn't say he was scared to die . . . nothing like that. No, he just put it out that he flatly refused to die. It's like the concept of death simply didn't apply to him. He wasn't having any of it. He said, "I will get through this. We will get through this." As if in giving it voice he would make it so.

I could only answer in kind. I said, "You're a survivor, man. Whatever life throws at you, you find a way to survive."

But underneath, I knew. Underneath, I had this sick, sad feeling that this was the last conversation we would ever have. When we were done talking, we embraced. Wasn't a typical thing for us. My father wasn't the most demonstrative man. But he was weak and I wanted to be strong for both of us, so I leaned over and collected him in a hug. Next thing I knew, I was bawling like a baby. So much for wanting to be strong. I was flat-out sobbing. His pillow was soaked through with my tears.

I'd never cried with my father before. It was cathartic as hell, terrifying as hell. And as I wept, I realized I had never really been alone with him, vulnerable with him, myself with him. It was just the two of us in his room, and it felt alien to me for it to be just the two of us like that. In all our times together, going back as far as I could remember, there was always another sibling around, or someone who worked for him, or one of his friends. There was always something else going on. His life was so damn big he had to fill it with people, and even now, he died as he lived. And yet there we were, father and son, lost in the desperate sadness of his one epic embrace, holding on to whatever it was we'd had, whatever it was I'd wished we had.

I can still remember the last of those distress calls from Grace when I was shuttling back and forth to Ibiza. I was having dinner at a place called Cafe Mambo with MSTRKRFT—Jesse Keeler and Al-P.

A rare photo of my immediate family. Also rare: we're all smiling.

I was always my mother's favorite. 😉

‣ My dad could beat your dad at backgammon.
‣ Who else can curl their tongue like my pops?
‣ My grandfather loved to play the ponies. Here we are at Hollywood Park.

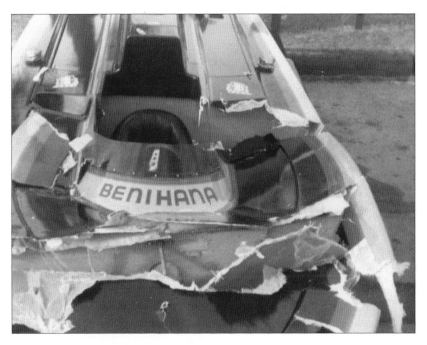

If you can believe it, this boat was in better shape than my father after his crash.

‣ Me and my brother Kevin when he was sent off to military school for causing too much trouble. (I still looked up to him.)

‣ My dad's spooky house in New Jersey.

‣ If you don't believe me when I say I was a scrawny little Asian kid, here's the proof. This poor girl wasn't my girlfriend or anything— just a classmate who was probably forced to dance with me because I was so pathetic.

The worst job of my life? Peeling nearly five hundred onions every morning at Benihana.

Regrets?

• Screaming my face off at a Civ show when they covered a Gorilla Biscuits song.

• One of Goodhue's first shows—at my buddy Andreas's house, in his parents' living room.

• This was the shot from that night when Farside called me up on stage to sing "Hero."

With This Machine Kills, at the Biko co-op in Isla Vista.

‣ The first Aoki jump?

‣ Here's the shot from that Box Packers show I wrote about, just before the cops came to shut us down. (They clearly didn't have the Christmas spirit.)

‣ The tools of the trade. Acoustic guitar? . . . check. Tea? . . . check. My lyric book? . . . check.

‣ Bread and Circuits, live at the Pickle Patch. Yes, it's a living room, and I'm taking the photo from the kitchen. (RIP Mike Kirsch.)

‣ In front of the legendary "Pickle Patch"—aka, "My Apartment." There are too many in this pic to ID, but I def need to ID my dog Kawaii.

‣ In front of what we called the "Pickle Frat." When we got kicked out of our Pickle Patch apartment for making too much noise, we took over an abandoned frat house on campus and made too much noise there.

My first computer—and the bunk bed I shared with Mike Phyte at the Pickle Patch, circa 1997. For what it's worth, this was all the furniture we could fit in our room.

‣ Driving The Kills across the USA, listening to Captain Beefheart nonstop.

‧ On the road with The Kills.

Tomorrowland, 2017: Music doesn't give a shit if you're black, white, gay, straight, Muslim, Jewish, Christian. It breaks down every border. We are all one. *(@caesarsebastian)*

White Raver Rafting— at Hakkasan in Las Vegas. *(@caesarsebastian)*

"Raise your hands if you're ready for some cake!" —on my home turf at Wet Republic. *(@caesarsebastian)*

▲ When I was in Kanye's orbit. *(Mark Hunter)*

▾ Lends new meaning to the "Cake Me!" chant. At Madame Tussauds. *(@caesarsebastian)*

▲ In Miami to promote our song "Azukita," flanked by Play-N-Skillz, with Daddy Yankee and Elvis Crespo. *(@caesarsebastian)*

▾ I've always wanted to be in a boy band. With my 3 Are Legend coconspirators Dimitri Vegas and Like Mike. *(@caesarsebastian)*

‣ Look Ma, I made it! Such a sick shot—and it somehow wound up in the Smithsonian. I'm told that me and Grandmaster Flash are the only DJs to be on display, and that we fit right in, right next to Dorothy's ruby slippers and some old dinosaur bones. (@caesarsebastian)

‣ With my managers Matt Colon and Michael Theanne. These guys have had my back for over ten years. I'd trust them with my life—and, apparently, my career! So stoked that I get to work and play and grow with my best friends. Can't wait to see what the next ten years bring. (@caesarsebastian)

▴ You can go home again: here I am in front of my first L.A. apartment building, on De Longpre Avenue. I moved in right after college. The neighborhood was so sketchy, I lived next door to a dominatrix, a struggling screenwriter, and a bunch of hookers who used to walk their dogs at all hours as a cover. *(@caesarsebastian)*

▾ Commemorating the life and legacy of Chester Bennington, following the Linkin Park memorial show at the Hollywood Bowl. *(@caesarsebastian)*

・ Do you know how hard I had to look to find a home in Vegas with my image at the bottom of the pool? *(@caesarsebastian)*

・ A boy and his toys: there's always time for a snowboard lesson on my trampoline. *(@caesarsebastian)*

・ At home, trying to find the next hook before Banksy's snake gets to me too. *(@caesarsebastian)*

▲ In the Neon Future Cave, where the sausage gets made. It's all blue, baby! (*@caesarsebastian*)

◂ Sitting pretty with Louis Tomlinson, celebrating the release of our song "Just Hold On." (*@caesarsebastian*)

▾ With BTS, doing the quintessential Aoki Jump—check out the serious air. (*@caesarsebastian*)

I stepped away from the table to take the call.

Grace said, "We don't know if he's going to make it this time."

I hopped the next flight to New York and rushed to my father's side at NYU Medical Center. It didn't feel like the last time, as I raced from the airport to the hospital. It was only the next time—one on a long string of many. And yet when I got to the hospital I was struck by all the tubes running into my father's mouth, his arms. It's like they had to plug him in to keep him ticking. He was mostly out of it, and I remember thinking how much he'd hated to be drugged, how important it was for him to feel like he was inside the moment, in some sort of control.

We stayed by his bedside in shifts. It was important to us that one of his children be with him at all times, and it just worked out that my turn on the night shift came on the night he passed. I didn't sleep. I sat in a chair next to his bed, holding his hand. I didn't read, didn't listen to music, didn't do anything but dwell inside that moment where my father used to be.

I didn't even pray. Not in the typical ways people pray. Not in the ways I might have prayed back in high school, when my acid-fueled epiphany had briefly turned me to religion—you know, the ways that might have placed me on God's insurance plan. No, whatever prayers I said in my head that night were the prayers of wish fulfillment. I was hoping against hope, that's all. Holding on for dear life to the one "higher power" who had stood before me like a force of nature from the very first time I went with him to one of his restaurants.

As I squeezed my father's hand, I imagined he was squeezing back. We sat in this way for five hours . . . six . . . seven . . . I talked to him, asked him questions about his life, about how things were for him in Japan, how things were when he met my mother, and I believed I heard his answers in his grip. In reality, his hand lay limp in mine, but I could have sworn he was holding on, tight, trying to tell me something.

At some point, around sunrise, I noticed a foul smell. It was my father, of course—he'd shit the bed. Like a hopeful idiot, I thought it was a positive sign. I took it to mean that his body was fighting back, trying to break through the tubes and the meds and the sickness, to eliminate the toxins, to get back to the business of living. I dressed it up in my head to mean more than it did, where in reality he wasn't fighting back so much as shutting down.

When I went to find one of the night nurses to tell her what was going on, she put it to me plain—said, "His organs are failing. It's only a matter of time."

I refused to hear her, asked to talk to a doctor. I said, "Yo, my dad's a fighter. He'll make it, you'll see."

The doctor tried once more to set me straight—said, "I'm surprised he's made it this far."

With this, I broke down. My entire body sagged. It's like all the air was let out of my lungs. I fell back into my chair and cried, and I switched into zombie autopilot mode. I started calling my siblings, told them to get back to Dad's room, told them it was the end. I wasn't thinking, just doing. I was drained of all emotion.

I wish I could remember what I said.

I wish I could remember what they said.

Next thing I knew, there they were. There *we* were. All of us. My father's fantastically blended family, stuck to him in all these different ways, saying our separate good-byes . . . together. Devon had taken the time to write her thoughts on a napkin, a scrap of paper, and when my father passed she looked at her notes and said a few words. She looked at him and said, "It's okay, you can go now. We're okay, you can go now."

Her words made my father's death real. All that "time of death" shit, all that doctor shit, it hadn't really registered. I knew, but I didn't *know* . . . if that makes any sense. And yet hearing our new truth from the lips of my kid sister, it finally hit me. Full in the chest. Hard. I was like, Holy shit, he's gone.

Today, I see my father in my siblings. His memory is most alive when we are together . . . all of us, some of us.

In my brothers and sisters, I see his many moods, his many colors, all these different pieces of his personality.

In my sister Grace I see my father's selflessness. She's always thinking about others, trying to set things right for the people in her life. A lot of folks, they hear me attach a word like *selfless* to my father, they wonder what the hell I'm talking about, but he was in the hospitality business, right? Whatever valves he might have shut off in his personal life, whatever ways he might have struggled with issues of intimacy or fidelity, he opened those spigots wide when it came to his work. He was an incredible host. He was generous, wanted to make people feel comfortable in his presence, and I see these qualities in Grace as well.

In my brother Kevin, I see my father's work ethic. More than any one of us kids, Kevin is on the grind. It's in his bones, same way it was with Dad. Me, I'm a hard-charger, but it's not the same. With me, it's mostly about being tireless. With Kevin, it's about being relentless. I'll fly to the edges of the planet to do a show without even thinking about it, but it's Kevin who's out there all day, every day, putting in the steady, meticulous work of getting things done. He's the operations guy of our crew, making sure the pieces all fit and the engine keeps running. He keeps the lights on for us.

In my sister Echo, I see my father's heart. Yeah, he could be hard on us kids, and he didn't always treat the women in his life—our mothers!—with the respect they deserved, but underneath his tough exterior he was a generous soul. He was good to the people who worked for him, good to people in need. Echo's cut the same way.

In my brother Kyle, I see my father's sense of humor. Kyle's the comedian of the family, only he goes at it in a take-no-prisoners sort of way. My father loved to make people laugh, but even more than that he loved to push their buttons, to make a situation so awkward or uncomfortable that you had to really pay attention. Kyle's like that, in his own way . . . in my father's way.

In my sister Devon, I see my father's mind. She's the brains of the outfit, smart as hell, always thinking ten steps ahead of everyone else. That was my father. It's like he was playing chess and everyone else was playing checkers, and with Devon you get the feeling she knows what's about to happen *way* before it up and happens. She can read the hell out of a room.

In my sister Jennifer, I see the close-knit family my father seemed to always want for himself but could never quite pull off. He was too distracted, too busy, to stay in any one place for any stretch of time, and so his family relationships suffered. But Jenny's built this wonderful family dynamic, and she's super-tight with her husband and kids, and I get the feeling that if my father had ever been able to get his shit together in this department, this would have been his model.

Me, I like to think I'm the DJ of all that Rocky Aoki DNA. I've got a little bit of all these character traits running through me. I've got all his little bits and pieces running through me, and I try to sample them all. I live each day trying to honor the man he was, the man I hope to become.

DROP

I always have a pair of jeans going.

It isn't the same pair, reaching all the way back to high school, but there's one pair in heavy rotation. You probably have a pair just like it. The feel . . . the color . . . the fit . . . you wear them out till they're just right. And when that happens . . . oh, man, you're good.

Don't know about you, but when I get my jeans right I won't take them off. These days, I might trick out my look with patches or a couple of tears, but the look is pretty much the same. You work those jeans in and wear them out until they turn that slate-gray/blue color that makes it look like you've been through some shit.

Do you know the color blue I mean? It's not the crisp, clean denim blue you take home from the store. It's the faded dirt blue that looks like it's been rubbed raw, the fabric feeling thin and soft and worn, the jeans running from dark to light and dark, the way you might see the ridge of tire tracks grooved into the earth in a dirt driveway.

It's a color that's been around.

I had a pair of jeans like that in high school. My mom was always on me to wash them, told me I should let her get me a new pair, but I loved the way they fit like they'd been painted on, like they were a part of me. Loved the way they looked, most of all. Like the most natural thing in the world.

Had another pair just like it around the time I was flying

*in and out of New York to visit my father in the hospital. I
can remember sitting in that straight-backed chair beside
his bed, nursing the rips in the fabric where the denim had
started to fray. Grabbing a pen from my bag and doodling
on the washed-out denim canvas of my thighs.*

*That faded blue of a worn pair of jeans . . . it's not a
color you see in nature. It's the color of hard work, and
perseverance, and not giving a shit. It's the color of time.*

Feelin' near as faded as my jeans . . .

*You know that line, I'm betting. It's imprinted on the
American songbook—"Me and Bobby McGee." You hear
it come around on that classic rock station and think what
it means to create a piece of poetry or a piece of music
that seeps into the culture and echoes across the
generations.*

*You close your eyes and picture the faded blue of the
pants you've been riding back and forth to Spain,
crisscrossing the planet, chasing the legacy of a man who
built an empire and pumped up the family name. A man
who lays dying in the bed next to you, whose very breath
falls into a sweet, staccato beat that starts to feel like it's
been synched to the very machines he's hooked up to.*

*I scratch a line or two of blue ink into the fabric, a
geometric shape, as I listen to the labored rhythm of my
father's breathing.*

*We are beaten down by these sad, low moments. We
are hardened, bone-weary.*

We are feeling blue.

9

WE'RE ALL A LITTLE SICK

I broke the edge after college.

For whatever reason, the straight-edge lifestyle began to lose its appeal. Can't say why, can't say how. I was still deep into the hardcore scene, totally immersed. All my friends, that's what they were into, but the idea that I had allowed myself to become defined by the fact that I didn't do drugs or drink alcohol didn't make sense to me anymore.

It was who I was at one point. It wasn't anymore.

It was a gradual regression, and I share it here because it leads to the downward spiral that found me after my dad's death. It started when I was living in another co-op off campus called Biko, named for Stephen Biko, the anti-apartheid activist from South Africa. There were a bunch of co-ops in and around Santa Barbara filled with vegetarians and activists, and Biko was my next stop along the way. I needed to stay in town after graduation to complete my last few credits, so I enrolled in a couple classes at Santa Barbara City College and threw in with this whole new group of personalities.

You have to realize, other than that one senseless acid trip I'd taken when I was a kid, I'd never touched drugs. I'd never taken a sip of alcohol. And now that I'd started to lose the *feel* for being clean and sober and totally in the moment now that the pure straight-edge piece of my lifestyle didn't seem so important, I had no idea what I was doing. And yet it's not like I was on completely unfamiliar ground. I'd been around kids who drank and smoked my whole life. I even used to invite these hippies who lived next door to me to smoke in my room. They thought it was weird, but they liked the idea of holding these bong rip parties in a straight-edge kid's room. It's like they were trespassing, stepping where they didn't belong. They had these enormous bongs—like, unnecessarily huge!—and they'd stand them up on the floor of my room while I pretended to study. I had no desire to smoke with them, but I loved the smell of marijuana, and the chill vibe these guys gave off when they were high. Also, I loved how serious they were about all of their equipment. They were like mad scientists setting up in their lab! Of course, looking back, I now realize I was probably stoned from all that secondhand smoke, but at the time I thought I was still doing my straight-edge thing.

Wasn't until I was a couple months into my "postcollege" days at Biko that I took my first drink. I was the same hardcore kid at heart. I kept staging shows at Biko, which had quickly become the new iteration of the Pickle Patch—Pickle Patch 2.0!—and one of the bands that came through was Kill Sadie. I'd just put out their album on Dim Mak, and we were all good friends—a bunch of straight-edge guys who'd already broken the edge. I was pumped that they were coming to town. They had a lot of cred in our little community. On the music front, they bounced around a lot, kept morphing into all these different bands, all these different groupings. Out of Kill Sadie, they formed Minus the Bear, which became a very popular band for a while, and then out of that they became Pretty Girls Make Graves, that band I'd signed to Dim Mak. But at the time I was mostly focused on breaking out of the shell I'd made for myself, and I was looking forward to having some fun with these guys.

So I did. We partied hard. Whatever my Kill Sadie pals were drinking, I was drinking—only I had no idea what they were drinking or how much of it I could handle. I ended up puking all over this beautiful vegetable garden that was like the heart of our co-op. Oh, man . . . I was such a loser, such a lightweight. Kill Sadie had this one song called "A Ride in the Centrifuge," and this was kind of like that. I felt like I'd been whipped around in some giant thrill ride and tossed onto the pavement. The guys I lived with wanted to kick me out of the house for that, because we grew our own vegetables, and to them it was like I'd just taken a shit on their lifestyle, but I managed to talk my way back into their good graces and stay on until I finished out the semester.

By the time I moved to Los Angeles a couple months later, I'd learned to hold my liquor. I began to understand why people would go to a bar to drink and socialize. There was something about the way the alcohol would lubricate the situation, get the conversation flowing, make the rest of the world melt away. Things were just so much easier with a drink or two, so much sweeter. It was like a whole new world opened up to me, and whatever awkwardness or shyness I still carried from those outside-looking-in days back in high school seemed to disappear as well. I wasn't a heavy drinker, although I can see now that I was laying the foundation. I hadn't exactly gone from zero to sixty, but I was cruising at a pretty good clip. Those first couple years after school, when I was ramping things up at Dim Mak and getting things started as a DJ, I'd have a drink from time to time. I'd have a bunch of drinks from time to time.

Wasn't any kind of big deal . . . until, at last, it was.

I don't think I realized it—in fact, I'm sure I didn't—but I'd gone from a casual drinker to a drinker, and the difference was everything. It started to feel like I couldn't get in the DJ booth without a drink or two before my sets, just to help me lose my inhibitions, and then that drink or two became two or three, then three or four. My go-to in those days was vodka and Red Bull. At first, I was a Jack-and-Coke guy, because that's what my friends used to drink, but I realized I needed an extra jolt of energy. When I started drinking, alcohol had mostly a soporific effect. It'd make me more tired than drunk. I needed to feel lit, alive, energized, so I switched things up and hit on this Red Bull cocktail. The vodka would slow me down, and the Red Bull would jack me up, and it was all good.

I was firing!

Over time, though, my drinking got out of hand. Here again, I don't think I realized it . . . but there it was. I started traveling to a ton of shows all over the world, mostly on my own, and the booze would keep me company. I didn't really know anybody in all these out-of-the-way places, so each time I hit a new town I'd grab a drink and try to fit myself in. I started drinking more and more, harder and harder. I didn't think of myself as an alcoholic or anything, but that had mostly to do with the fact that I wasn't thinking. I was just doing. And in a lot of ways, I *was* doing okay—I didn't miss a show, didn't miss a beat, but I did miss a flight or two—like that time Matt and I slept through the gate announcements on our way to the Super Bowl after-party. Another time, I was so hungover I ended up missing *two* flights on the same leg. I fell asleep in front of my gate and missed the first flight, but then when I got it together to get myself rebooked and checked in for another flight, I passed out again and missed the second flight. I was laid out—and, yeah, I was exhausted from all the travel I was doing, but the drinking didn't help.

I wouldn't say I was spiraling out of control, but I was certainly spiraling. And I wasn't in control of shit. I wasn't myself. And the whole time I was shuttling back and forth to be at my father's side in the hospital, I was drinking. I'd gone from never touching a drop of alcohol to feeling like I needed it to keep me going.

It was a dark time in my life and in the life of my family, and as I was diving deeper into the DJ scene, I started to feel all this pressure. Just to be clear, it was a self-inflicted kind of pressure, but as I was playing to bigger and bigger crowds, it felt to me like I was really pushing it. I was on the road constantly, afraid to slow down, afraid to stop and think about the choices I was making. My thing was to keep moving, you know. To stay busy. The road was my new life, my new friend, my new reality.

This was the ride I was on, and there was no getting off.

All that touring, all that drinking . . . it cost me a long-term relationship with my girlfriend at the time. It cost me a little bit of momentum and focus at Dim Mak. It got in the way of how things were with my family. It started to fuck with my health, my head. I was just a complete mess, and things would get worse before they got better.

Way worse.

About a year after my father died, I lost another someone close to me—my great friend DJ AM, rest in peace, was found dead in his New York City apartment from an apparent drug overdose. More than anyone else in and around the LA music scene, in and around the DJ scene, it was Adam who encouraged me, inspired me. I hit this earlier, but I want to hit it harder here. We were inseparable for a while—but then, as I started traveling, we kind of splintered off in our own directions. We each had these relentless, ridiculous schedules, and underneath all that craziness I suppose there was always the thought that we would reconnect whenever life and career put us in the same place at the same time.

Only that's not exactly how things shook out. AM had a history of drug addiction. He used to speak openly about it. He'd tried to kill himself at one point early on in his career, and he spoke about that, too. He'd been sober the entire time I knew him, when we were close. He was in AA, and he took it seriously, but you could see he had this obsessive personality. If you were at his house, for example, and he liked a certain cereal, you could open one of the kitchen cabinets and find, like, ten boxes of the stuff. If he liked a certain shoe . . . ten pairs. Everything with AM was extreme, in excess.

He was like a mentor to me. A life coach. Every time I had a problem, he'd talk me through it. Didn't matter what time it was. Didn't matter what he had going on. He'd stop whatever he was doing and listen. I'd never had a friend like that before—he was so selflessly and endlessly available to me, and I used to wonder if he thought of me in the same way. But then our lives went off in these different directions and the dailiness went out of our friendship. We'd still talk from time to time, and we'd get together when we were nearby, but it wasn't the same—and it weighed on me that it wasn't the same.

Next thing I knew, the news broke that he was in a plane crash—a Learjet 60 he was in overran a runway in South Carolina and crashed into an embankment and burst into flames. There were six people on board. AM and Travis Barker were the only survivors.

AM was shaken by the incident. Travis, too—he swore off flying after that. Their friends were affected as well. I'd just played a show with the two of them, so I started to think it could have been me on that plane. I was having all these crazy *what if?* thoughts—couldn't shake 'em. AM and Travis were both severely burned in the crash, so I drove down to the burn center immediately to see them. I saw Travis first. He was up and lucid, told me the whole story. What a fucking nightmare! Such sadness! Then I walked down the hall to see AM, and he was still out of it. He had this wild Spider-Man–type net over his face, was hooked up to an IV. His arms looked like the pigskin of a football. I broke down, seeing him like that. Seeing him *here*, like that. Walking up and down the hallways of this unit, you'd see the worst kind of burn victims. It was gruesome, horrifying. But there was something about seeing my friend like that, looking like an open wound, that I just couldn't handle. I don't mean to make the moment seem like it was all about me, because it wasn't like that, but I started to see myself in that hospital bed. Those crazy *what if?* thoughts were front and center.

AM was in such tremendous pain when he came to, and he had his AA sponsor there with him, to kind of coach him through the pain meds dilemma. I remember AM was torn up about having to take pain medication. He'd been clean for so goddamn long, he didn't want to lose that feeling of strength that came with all those years of sobriety, but at the same time the pain was just unbearable.

He needed those meds, of course, but they set him off on another downward spiral. He started using again. Weed, crack . . . whatever. He stiff-armed his friends, his AA sponsor, kept saying he had it together, just needed this one day, this one week, to burn this desire out of his system, and then he'd start the clock again on being clean. Saying he could get his shit back together at any time. Saying it was all good.

Aw, fuck . . . it breaks my heart to revisit all of this, because we'd been so tight, but we kind of went off in our separate directions again after Adam was released from the burn unit. I went back to doing my own thing, consumed by what was going on with my father, and AM was just trying to get his life back together, build himself back up. When the news broke about his death, the first reports said police had found a crack pipe at his side, and toxicology reports later showed that he had traces of cocaine, oxycodone, hydrocodone, clonazepam, and a slew of other drugs in his system.

I was devastated—flattened, really. We were like brothers, the two of us, and I felt so fucking guilty that I hadn't been there for him in the months leading to that plane crash, in the months after. I'd been so swallowed up by my own shit, I couldn't see the shit my friend was dealing with . . . and now he was gone. It killed me that I hadn't been there for him, killed me that all these chunks of time had gone by where I hadn't even *thought* of him, that's how swallowed up I was by what was going on with me. In my head, I had it fixed that I was barreling toward success, and nothing would get in the way of that. Nothing would stop this wave I told myself I was riding. Not the loss of my father. Not the financial struggles we were having at Dim Mak. Not the alcohol. Nothing. And now, with Adam gone like that, it forced me to reflect on the way I was living.

I realized I hadn't really talked to anyone in my family since my father had died.

I hadn't spent any time with my mom.

I didn't have a girlfriend—or any type of stable, steadying relationship.

I was unmoored, bouncing from one gig to the next and hoping blindly, stupidly, that the direction I was headed in was the direction I was meant to be going.

Like I said, I was a complete fucking mess, so as soon as I processed the news of Adam's death, as soon as I ran out of tears, I swore off drinking.

Cold stop.

It was the only way I knew to get my head right. I didn't swear off alcohol entirely, because I'd still take a sip in celebration or on a special occasion, but what I was able to chase immediately was the *urge* to drink. The feeling that I needed to drink to get by . . . *that's* what left me when AM died, and to this day I'm grateful that I was able to step away from that urge so easily.

Yep, Adam's death was my wake-up call. And it's not like I lifted myself from these low, low moments and decided to embrace the straight-edge lifestyle again. No, the term had lost its meaning for me. The scene had lost its meaning. But what meant something to me still was this hard-won determination to live clean, to live healthy.

Meant everything, actually.

Long as I'm on it, I want to spend some time here on two other deaths that left me reeling—two deaths that stand as reminders of the knife-edge we sometimes walk when we spend our lives on the road, chasing approval, acceptance, validation . . . whatever it is that drives us in the music business. Doesn't matter if you're a DJ or a musician or a roadie . . . there are pressures that attach to the fast-paced touring lifestyle, there are demons, and those pressures and demons only get bigger when you mix in drugs and alcohol.

It gets to you, the constant need to give the fans a good time, to lift them from the routine of their daily lives and give them a shot of energy and excitement, even if you're feeling shitty. Even if you're kept from your own routines.

Now, I don't pretend to understand what it means to be clinically depressed. I don't understand the black funk people slip into when they're feeling lost or suffocated. That shit's way beyond my pay grade, you know—and, mercifully, way beyond my experience. But I get it. I do. I've looked down that rabbit hole a time or two when I was lost in the fog of drink, when I was feeling tired and broken and lonely and slapped around by the road. No, I was never so far gone that I ever thought about killing myself, but I could see how those thoughts might look. I could play that scene out and imagine the combustion of moment and mindlessness that would allow them to appear.

Tragically, the road is littered with stories of artists who struggle with depression, fall to depression. Sometimes, those stories hit way too close to home . . .

I first heard about Chester Bennington's death in a text message. I was sitting on my bed in a hotel room in New York, in the middle of a long slog of my own. Feeling bone-tired, alone. The message didn't make any sense to me at first. I'd seen Chester not that long ago. He seemed healthy, happy. He was in the middle of a major tour for Linkin Park's new album, *One More Light*. By all outward appearances, it looked like he was crushing it, riding high.

I thought, *This can't be right*. I thought, *No fucking way*.

I called my manager, Matt, to see if he had any information. He was always plugged into the news as it happened. And it took talking it through for a while with Matt for me to get my head around the news. Chester was such a singular talent. A special talent. One of the most compelling voices in music.

I got off the phone with Matt and buried my head in my pillow. I was overcome, overwhelmed. I'd known Chester for only five or six years, but that was more than enough time to come to love him, admire him, respect the hell out of him. We'd worked together on a couple songs, performed together a couple times, flitted in and out of each other's lives for a while. I was overwhelmed by the sadness of it, the cruelty of it. The *nearness* of it, if that makes sense. What struck me most of all was how his death would destroy his wife, his kids . . . his great friend Mike Shinoda. The rest of the band, too—they were all so tight. I wept for them and for the millions of Linkin Park fans around the world. It was such a heartbreak—and then, when it was reported that Chester's death was a suicide, I lost it all over again, because in this one desperate act I could see a hundred others.

Soon as I had my shit together, I sent a text to Mike, told him how fucking sorry I was. Told him I was here for him and the rest of the guys in the band. Told him it felt like I'd lost a piece of my heart.

Somewhere in there I took the time to give thanks that I'd been able to step away from alcohol in time to get my head straight, because part of me feared what I would do if I ever felt desperately lost or alone when there were a couple bottles at hand.

I went back into the studio after Chester died and opened up the stems on the two songs we'd done together with Linkin Park—"Darker Than Blood" and "A Light That Never Comes." I got lost all over again in the music we made together. It ended up that I made a new drop for "A Light That Never Comes," and then I did a mash-up of the two songs and started playing them in my sets. It meant the world to me, to be able to channel my emotions into my music . . . into Chester's music. And to donate all the proceeds from those songs to the One More Light Fund, which the band was setting up.

A couple weeks later, Mike Shinoda called and told me about a benefit the band was putting together at the Hollywood Bowl in Chester's memory. He asked if I could make it, and of course I agreed. I canceled whatever shows I had going on for that date, and flew in for the concert—from Kentucky, I think. Somehow, I kept it together enough to perform "A Light That Never Comes," with Bebe Rexha joining me onstage to sing the Chester parts. I also dropped a new remix for "One More Light," this achingly sad Linkin Park song. It's such a beautiful, powerful ballad, and it was one of the great blessings of my career to be able to reimagine it in this *new* light, for Chester, and as I played it for the first time that night, I was struck by the way the song seemed to foreshadow Chester's death. It was like a love letter to a wounded soul who was maybe feeling lost and suicidal, telling him or her to hang on, not lose hope.

Who cares if one more light goes out?
In a sky of a million stars
It flickers, flickers

To this day, I'm still playing that remix to close out some of my sets, and each time out I have to fight back tears. Each time, I think what it would have meant to have a chance to play that song for Chester a final time—maybe get him to see the warmth and wisdom in his words in a way that might have lifted him from the darkness.

Such a voice. Such a talent. Such a loss.

Tim Bergling was a different kind of animal.

He wasn't built for a life on the road, a life on a public stage. He was an incredible musician, a gifted songwriter, a beautiful singer. He understood music theory and composition . . . one of those rare talents who could do it all. But unlike, say, Prince, Tim was working in the EDM space, where his talents as a producer were just as impressive as his musicianship.

He was in the studio constantly. He was a complete master of his craft—one of the most influential figures in EDM, period.

Hell, he's the reason EDM even exists, and it just worked out that as dance music seeped into our festival culture, it dragged Tim along with it. As the trend-stamping DJ Avicii, he was at the heart of an evolution in EDM, where the DJ started to command attention, and he wasn't cut out for that shit. Tim would have been the first to tell you how nervous he'd get every time he had to do a set. And it was more than just nerves, he sometimes said. It was an uneasiness, a disquiet. He felt out of his element. But he was just so fucking good at what he did that he couldn't escape the pull of the stage.

Tim was making music as Avicii almost from the time I started working in that space, but he was just a kid. I can remember him turning up at one of our Dim Mak Sundays parties at Drai's Hollywood when he was just nineteen or twenty years old. In those days, he was putting out records on this underground Australian label called Vicious—and even then you could tell he was special. There was something introspective, poetic, kinetic about his music—you knew right away when you were in the grip of an Avicii song.

We did this tour together in 2011 called Identity Festival, which was around the time Avicii exploded with his hit song "Levels." That song was as big as it gets—the anthem of anthems. He was just white-hot in those days, and he stayed white-hot—really, he was such a brilliant creative force. We bonded on that tour, kept talking about ways we might collaborate in the future. In fact, just before he died, I was working on a track I was planning to send to him, just to get his take—it felt to me like the perfect song for us to work on together.

But I never got around to it.

I was riding in the backseat of an Uber in New York when my phone started blowing up with the news that he was gone. It was April 2018. Avicii was just twenty-eight years old. I was devastated. The first reports didn't say anything about suicide, but I had an idea. Not because he'd ever said anything. He was such a dynamic presence— he lit up every room he was in!—but at the same time you could see he was tortured, troubled. He seemed to move inside this magical force field, while he himself never appeared all that comfortable, especially when he was on stage, performing.

My most cherished memory of Avicii cuts against this idea that he was out of his element when he was on stage. We were at the Tomorrowland festival, in Belgium, which I had closed out for the past bunch of years. Avicii was playing in the second-to-last slot, just before me on the main stage. For whatever reason, I always got a case of the nerves when I played that festival. It made no sense: I'd been in that featured spot for five years, and yet it still had me on edge.

Well, this one year, Avicii came backstage after his set and noticed I was a little out of it. He was good about that—plugged in to the people around him, to the mood of the room.

He'd always been open about his own jitters as a performer, so I figured I could come clean with him. I said, "Don't know what it is, Tim. I've played this festival a million times, but I'm nervous as hell."

Just putting it out there made me feel a little better.

Avicii just looked at me and flashed this wide, welcoming smile. He didn't say a word, just kept grinning, so I kept talking—said, "I'm freaking out, man. I'm, like, not ready to play."

As I was yammering, Avicii was walking over to me, still smiling. When he reached me, he collected me in a giant bear hug—picked me right up off the floor and squeezed tight, like he was hugging the fear right out of me.

And, in a way, he was. Drawing it right out of me and perhaps reclaiming it for himself.

My photographer Caesar Sebastian was with me backstage that night and he happened to capture the moment—it's one of my favorite pictures. I put it up on Instagram, and people really responded to it. In a single shot, it told a bunch of stories. It told a story of how the pressures of touring and performing can get to you, even if you've been down this road before. It told a story of how a young visionary set aside his own fears and generously offered to swallow up mine, once the weight of performing his own set had been lifted.

Mostly, it told the story of this giant of a performer who was never quite himself on stage but who went out of his way to ease his friend's suffering.

When you lose someone close to you, someone who's had a big influence on you, it pushes you to reexamine things, maybe look a little longer, a little deeper, at some of the ways you've been living. Me, I was a complete fucking mess in the early stages of my career as a DJ. It's a wonder I had any career at all. It's only now that I can see I wasn't doing everything I could to connect with my fans. In fact, you could even say I was doing everything I could to keep them at a distance. It wasn't them . . . it was *me*. They were fully invested in what I was putting out there—the music, the energy, the emotion—but a part of me was holding back. You can't give of yourself entirely when you're shit-faced half the time. When you're phoning it in instead of being dialed-in, the way I am now.

I didn't realize it at the time, but my early shows had no essence to them . . . no heart . . . no personality. I couldn't put myself into what I was doing, because I was hiding in the fog of being drunk. The way it worked with me, when I was drunk, all my emotions were exaggerated. If I was really happy, I'd kick it up to super fucking happy. If I was depressed, I'd take it down to super fucking depressed. The alcohol would just spank me around and drag me to this place of extremes, and what that meant when I was performing was that I'd get stuck inside this bubble of my own making, surrounded by a swirl of emotions that had nothing to do with the audience and everything to do with whatever was going on in my own head. I couldn't see beyond that, so it made sense that my fans couldn't *see* me.

All that time breathing in my own air, I couldn't really touch what was right in front of me, what was to the side of me. I had no situational awareness, was simply filling the spaces where I was playing with sound and noise, which for a DJ is like the kiss of death. My head was so far up my own butt, there's no way I could have picked up on what these crowds were putting out. All I cared about was the music I was playing, when my focus should have been on what the people in the crowd were *hearing*. And do you know what? As soon as I quit drinking, I was able to shift my focus, and play my music with intention. I'd pick out people in the crowd and play to them. I'd look into their eyes, take in their expressions, try to imagine myself in their experience. I started thinking like a sociologist, wondering how this or that fan might respond to the feelings embedded in a song, in a hook, in a snatch of lyric.

Connectivity . . . that became my thing. Should have been my thing all along, but I didn't have the head for that when I was drinking.

Straight-edge or not, I needed to keep a clear head if I wanted what I was doing to matter.

DROP

I am alone.

Cue the fucking violins, right? I mean, I live in a big house, play to big crowds, live a big, full life. But, end of the day, it sometimes feels my life is empty. In the movie of my life that's been playing in my head since I was a kid, I always have a family. I am a father. And yet in my reality I'm forty years old, and it should have happened for me by now. Truth is, I've been chasing this career so damn long, so damn hard, there's no room in it for a white picket fence. There is only the blue of loneliness, emptiness—the collateral damage of a life on the road, a life at full throttle. It's a price I've been willing to pay because I tell myself I have all the time in the world, but it's starting to feel like all the time in the world is running out on me. My father had six kids by the time he was my age, and even though he didn't offer any kind of positive template for how to raise a family, he was way ahead of where I am, and where I am is . . . nowhere.

Everywhere and nowhere, all at once . . .

Things almost fell another way, not too long ago. Remember how I wrote earlier that I don't always notice the color of people's eyes? Well, the one exception to that just about knocked me on my ass: the electric-blue gaze of an Australian woman I met when I was touring Down Under.

Her name was Tiernan, and I was smitten. Over the moon. Gone.

I was at a festival with Mark "Cobrasnake" Hunter, one of the most influential photographers on the underground LA party scene—same way the graphic artist So Me defined the look and feel of the Ed Banger movement out of France. He was my best friend and running buddy for about ten years when I was starting out. Everywhere I DJed, Cobrasnake was in tow, capturing the culture. He had a great eye, extraordinary vision, and here he was drawn to a stunning, blue-eyed blonde in pink Ksubi shorts. He said, "Oh, my God. That girl is gorgeous."

He was right. She was. She was also whip-smart, fun, kind, grounded. We ended up talking, traded numbers, stayed in touch. A year or so later, she flew out to Los Angeles.

Tiernan.

The one that got away.

Not before I married her, though. We got engaged about a month after she arrived in California. Wasn't anything going on in Australia that she was rushing to get back to, and we were caught in the swirl of romance, and it felt to us like the thing to do. It was exciting as hell. We didn't discuss a wedding date or anything—I hadn't even met her family! But the idea of spending the rest of my life with this woman was just so ridiculously appealing to me.

We were having fun, moving forward, seeing how our lives at each other's side might work.

It was a wild, thrilling ride.

Tiernan would go on the road with me a lot of the time. We took an apartment together on Hope Street in Los Angeles—how's that for wistful, wishful foreshadowing?

But then I looked up one day and realized we were no closer to getting married than we were when I proposed. We'd been together three, four, five years, and she was still rockin' the ring I'd given her, but I started to see all these little cracks in our relationship. Wasn't so easy to share a life like mine. I was traveling like a demon, and things had kicked up a couple notches in Tiernan's career, so she was off doing her thing as well. We moved in our own separate orbits. When we were together, life was good. When we were apart, there was tension. Tiernan was always on me to step off the runaway train we were riding, and it worked out that we were gifted the chance for a total reset when I had to power down for a major surgery to repair my vocal cords.

Backstory: I'd been struggling with my voice for some time. It would disappear on me, from all the screaming I'd do on stage. Then it would come back raspy and hoarse. I tried every conceivable remedy, until I finally went to a surgeon, who discovered a large nodule that needed to be removed. As part of my recovery, I'd have to keep still and quiet for about six weeks after the surgery, to allow my throat to heal.

I resisted the idea at first—just couldn't get my head around it. But Tiernan was all for it—said it would be good for us to dial things down and chill for a while. So that's what we did. I canceled a bunch of shows in Spain, the Netherlands, the UK—just wiped the slate clean. We used the time to do a full-body heal. I started meditating, eating right, taking piano lessons. It was an opportunity for us to work on our relationship, and for me to discover all these new outlets for my creativity. She just loved that I was stopping the train in this way, thought it would be good for me. Good for us. And it was. For a while.

We finally got married a couple months after my surgery—a kick-ass wedding in Hawaii later that year. All the trimmings. Her family. My family. Our friends . . . our own little royal wedding.

All along, we'd been in couples therapy, but one month after we were married the tone of those sessions started to change. I guess it took the two of us coming together in *front of all the people we cared about for things to finally fall apart. We were a mess, and out of respect to Tiernan and the relationship we shared I will keep the details of that mess private. However, what I will say is that we were headed in different directions, wanted different things.*

A line like that, it reads like a cop-out, I know. Like I've got something to hide. But that was the core: Tiernan wanted to be in New York, to pursue her career. I'd just built my house in the hills outside Las Vegas, overlooking the strip, so I wanted to be in Nevada.

Those idyllic days we'd spent in our apartment on the aptly named Hope Street in Los Angeles were forever out of reach.

And so I am back where I started. Alone. Wondering how it is that life can somehow pass you by when you're living large. I catch myself some nights, crying on the floor of a far-off hotel room, wondering what my life will be like at fifty, sixty, seventy. This is not me being melodramatic. This is me despairing. This is me being real. This is me filling the hole in my life where my movie-family is meant to be.

I have only shared these thoughts with a precious few people, but it feels right to share them here. I must be honest. I must admit to myself that I can't keep this pace forever—but then, I can't imagine anything else. The constant travel . . . the playing to millions of fans each year . . . the thrill-seeking . . . the white-hot excitement that finds me on the edges of our popular culture . . . it's all I know.

You know, on second thought, I suppose I have opened up about this with my fans, in my own way. Through my songs. When I think back on the past couple years since Tiernan and I split, I'm realizing that I'm making the best music of my career. I'm connected to my songs in the most personal way. I seem to be leaning away from the bangers and toward the more emotional pieces, like the song "Just Hold On." You can just see how it touches people's hearts. You can see it at my shows, or in the feedback that finds me online. No, I didn't write the lyrics to that one, but the music is uplifting, compelling, healing . . . all that good shit. And it comes from this dark, bleak place, where I sometimes get to feeling blue and lonely and like I am destined to travel through this life alone.

Hey, as long as you're suffering, you might as well turn it into art, right?

In my low, despairing moments, I catch myself thinking of my sister Devon and the choices she's made with her own life and career. It's easy to forget that there was a time when I was starting out and it was Devon who lived in the harsh light of celebrity. She was one of the top supermodels on the planet, and I was known as Devon Aoki's older brother. Oh, man . . . she was the shit. She was living the life I'm living now, but she had the courage (and the foresight!) to step away from it when the universe gave her a chance. She wasn't planning on starting a family, but when she got pregnant she took it as a gift. A sign. A reminder of what was important. She'd always known she wanted a family. And then there it was, hers for the taking, so she grabbed at it.

I'm happy for my sister. Really and truly. But I am envious, too. I want what she has. I want the universe to gift me the same opportunity. Maybe it already did, when it sent me Tiernan. Maybe it will again.

I can only hope.

While I'm waiting for fate to do its thing, I reach for the only family I know. My mother . . . my sisters . . . my brothers . . .

The reaching actually started with my cousin Taku. He's a few years older than me, and we'd never been close as kids, but I always looked up to him. He was kinda scary-looking, kinda intimidating, but he was hardcore, same as me. We didn't run in the same circles, but we listened to the same music. We were steeped in the same culture, and I followed what he was up to.

When I started Dim Mak I hit him up for the artwork to one of his tattoos. See, we were cousins on both sides—his father is my dad's brother; his mother is my mom's cousin—and he wore this crazy-sick piece that was like the Aoki–Kobayashi family crest. I hit him up and said, "I need this for my label. Send me the graphic." I loved how it represented both sides of the family, you know, thought we'd use it as some type of logo, maybe show how we're like the sum of all of our influences. So he sent me the artwork, but then we went a whole bunch of years where we didn't really see each other, didn't really speak to each other.

Taku was hiding out on the East Coast, working his own restaurants, doing his own thing, and when I played a gig in Atlantic City he came through. We hung out. He helped out, too. He's just one of those guys who pitches in, does whatever needs to be done without even being asked, and I needed someone like that on the road with me, so I put it to him plain—said, "You want to jump on tour with me?"

He said, "Fuck it, let's do something completely different."

So he put a pin in whatever he was doing with his restaurants and came out to Vegas with his wife, Cheryl, to work with me. It was great to be so connected, so close, to someone from my family. I'd been living on my own for so long, going through my own motions, that I'd forgotten what it was like to have someone around who shared your blood, your history. I started to think of ways to bring the rest of my family to Vegas as well.

I looked next to my mother. I wanted to take care of

her, have her near. I woke up one day and realized we were only in each other's lives in a surface way. There was no dailiness to our relationship, no connectivity. She was still living in Newport Beach, not far from my sister Grace and her family. So I told her I'd buy a house for her down the street. We could be neighbors. She was open to it but didn't want to leave Grace, so I put it out to my sister as well. A couple months later, they came back to me and said they were down. All in. Keep in mind, this was no easy thing for Grace and her husband, Brent. She worked as a therapist. He worked in IT. They had two teenage daughters—my nieces, Olivia and Natalie. They'd made a life for themselves in Newport Beach. But they were ready for something new, so I found a great house for them in my neighborhood where they could set up camp.

It's been a great blessing to reconnect with my family in this way. To reconstruct my family in this way. We are now a constant presence in each other's lives. When I'm home, I'm surrounded by family. When I'm on the road, I have people to come home to.

Understand, I've always been close to my mother, but it's been a closeness of affection and not connection. We don't always talk, or dig into each other's emotions. It is not the Japanese way, not my mother's way. But she's such a constant source of sweetness and light, and I'm oh so grateful to have her close. She looks out at the world from such a joyful place, it's infectious. Every day, she delights me in some magical way—like the time I caught her pinching a piece of ABC chewing gum (as in "already been chewed") from one of her kitchen drawers, and she could only shrug her shoulders, half-embarrassed, as she explained to me that it still had its flavor. Or the time she got tired of an old sweater she'd had forever so she ran a scissor down the front and turned it into a makeshift cardigan—saying, "Look, Steven! A new sweater!"

She's such a good sport when I chase after her with my phone and try to capture some piece of Mom silliness for my social media feed. The fans just love it—but even if they didn't, I'd go ahead and do it anyway, because it makes me happy. It makes my mother happy! I've even pulled her into the studio—had her drop a lyric on a psy-trance collab I did with Vini Vici called "Moshi Moshi." We gave her featured billing, as "Mama Aoki." (She's the star of the video!)

With Grace, it's different. With Grace, I can share what's going on in my life, in my head, and she can share the same with me. For years, I knew her only peripherally. She left for college when I was just a little kid, so we were moving on different planes. And now here we are in each other's lives in a full-on way—a great, good thing.

These days, I'm working on my brother Kevin to make a similar move. I want to grow this late-stage family to include all of my siblings, all of their families, and with Kevin the prospect is tied to a couple business deals we've got working. The biggest of these is a chain of Japanese restaurants we're developing—Aoki Teppanyaki, a reboot of what my father started with Benihana. We're hoping to pay homage to the style of cooking he helped to popularize, and to honor our heritage, but we'll give it a millennial spin. We're already open in Florida, and looking ahead to the opening of our flagship location in Las Vegas.

We've also got a chain of Bluetree Cafe locations up and running—in Miami, Vegas, and Shibuya, Japan. Here again, we're out to honor the Aoki tradition, with a health and wellness concept that features cold-pressed juices and teas and coffees, throwing back to the teahouses my grandfather used to run, shining new light on the Aoki name.

Ao . . . ki . . .

Blue. Tree.

With Kevin in the fold, I'll look next to Kyle, and see if I can't come up with some way to entice him to move to the desert. He's an aspiring filmmaker and musician, so I'm sure there are a ton of opportunities he can tap into in my adopted hometown.

I'm afraid my other sisters are pretty much entrenched where they are in their lives right now. Echo has her own career going on in the Bay Area, where she lives with her daughter, and Devon's doing her thing in Los Angeles. Jennifer's on the East Coast, running an incredible family business with her husband, so I won't be able to complete the Aoki compound anytime soon, but there'll be more and more opportunities for us all to be together with so many of us living so close.

In this way, I am reassembling the family I never really had. Filling the spaces where my own little family might someday be. No, it is not the same as having a wife and children of my own, but it is something.

For now, it is everything.

10

TURN UP THE VOLUME

Took me a while to find my voice as an artist.

I'd been looking for it all along, all the way back to when I was a kid trying to find my community, trying to think what it was that made me like a certain band or remember a certain show. It had to do with the music, but it also had to do with something I couldn't always describe. Something vague. Something ephemeral. Something beyond explaining.

Still, I tried to understand it. For the longest time, this was like a puzzle to be solved, trying to figure out why I'd felt such a gut connection to some of these artists, like this art band I loved called Men's Recovery Project. The group was made up of former members of other great bands I used to listen to—Sam McPheeters from Born Against; Neil Burke, from Life's Blood. They were hardcore, but they also had a postmodern absurdist streak that left you scratching your head and wondering what they were trying to say with their music. News of one of their very first shows went viral, back when *going viral* wasn't even a thing. It was more of an urban legend, and I've yet to meet anyone who was actually *at* that early show, but the stories about it are . . . well, *urban legendary*. The story goes that Sam and Neil and the rest of the band put up a bunch of flyers all over New York City, announcing a performance at 8:00 a.m. on a certain date, at a coffee shop. The coffee shop part wasn't all that strange—bands played in all kinds of un-likely places. But the 8:00 a.m. time was odd. I mean, who plays a show at eight o'clock in the morning?

Clearly, these guys were a little different. Nobody at the coffee shop knew anything about a Men's Recovery Project show. There was no sign outside, no flyers on the windows . . . nothing. A small crowd of forty or fifty people showed up, and Men's Recovery Project eventually came out. No instruments, no sound equipment . . . nothing. They sat down at an empty table—*and started eating cereal.*

That was the show: the guys in the band, eating cereal. What the fuck, right?

Keep in mind, I wasn't at that show, didn't know anybody who was at that show, but the story around it spread like a bizarre game of Tele-phone. People were talking about it—for the longest time, people were talking about it.

I went to see Men's Recovery Project when I was in high school, at the Huntington Beach Public Library. (See what I mean about bands playing in the unlikeliest places?) I'd heard about that infamous coffee shop gig in New York and wanted to see what they were up to, and when I got to the library the band had already set up and started play-ing. There was a small crowd, but nobody could see Sam McPheeters. We could hear him singing—the rest of the band, we could see them playing. But Sam McPheeters was nowhere to be seen, and then a group of us spied this super-long mic cord running from the front of the stage and down a super-long hallway. So we followed the cord . . . all the way to the bathroom! And there was Sam McPheeters, singing from the toilet seat in one of the stalls, and as soon as he was spotted he darted from the bathroom with a stiletto duct-taped to his face, screaming out of the side of his mouth.

I looked on and thought, *This is the craziest shit I've ever seen.* And when I think back on that show now, I don't remember the music. What I remember is the *wow*—the stuff I told my friends about the next day, and all the days after that.

Jump ahead a couple years to the Pickle Patch shows we staged in our living room in Santa Barbara. Somehow, Men's Recovery Project heard about us and wanted in. It all happened in this organic way. Folks would come by, and they'd be into it, and they'd go off and tell another group of folks, and they would come by, and so on. But Men's Recovery Project was at that point a semi-renowned underground art band, and I was pumped to be able to feature these guys.

The night they were due to play, we put the word out in our usual ways, and we maybe had thirty, forty people show up. We had another band in the lineup, Thrones, only Thrones wasn't really a band, just a solo project for this bass player named Joe Preston, who would eventually go on to play with Men's Recovery Project. (Just look at all the throughlines!) Thrones set up these six bass stacks, and he started creating this wild, pulsing, metal wall of noise. Joe Preston had a giant beard, and I was struck by how he carried himself—a really strange guy, playing really strange music, didn't give a shit what people thought.

After the Thrones set, we were all kind of waiting for Men's Recovery Project to come out, but they didn't have their equipment set up in the living room, and I had all these people pressed close together in this too-tight space. I started getting anxious about the time and the long wait. I was a fan, but I was also a promoter, so I had all these other elements to think about, couldn't really lose myself in the moment. I kept going over to Sam and them and saying, "Yo, you guys gotta get set to play," and they just kept shrugging me off.

Finally, after about a half hour, they walked in the front door— *completely fucking naked!* The drummer carried his drum kit in front of him. The guitarist had his guitar in front of him. The bass guitarist, same thing. They were all wearing masks. And then one of the guys walked to the mic stand someone had set up—the only piece of equipment that was ready to go—and dropped this giant bag of Twinkies and Yodels and chips and ham and all kinds of junk food on the floor in front of him. To this day, I couldn't tell you who was who or what was what, because they all had their masks on, but it was so completely outrageous and shocking and compelling as hell, what these guys were doing. One guy started grabbing a bunch of Twinkies and smearing them all over the ass of one of the other guys—crazy, loopy, thrilling stuff.

Totally *out there.*

Meanwhile, Sam McPheeters was also *out there*—meaning that he was waiting in the van outside, motor running, and after these guys were done bending each other over and doing all this foul, funny shit with the Twinkie cream, one of them stepped to the mic and said, "Hey, we're Men's Recovery Project."

Then they filed out of the house and into the van and drove off. And *that* was the show.

Men's Recovery Project wasn't the only band out there pushing the edges in this way. In the punk and hardcore world, there were a ton of artists challenging the conventions of music and performance. One of my favorite bands, Lightning Bolt, had a drummer who wore a ski mask with a microphone sewn into the fabric. And then there was this one performance artist, Chris Burden, who had someone shoot him in the shoulder with a rifle in one of his shows; in another, he crucified himself to the back of a Volkswagen Bug and had someone drive him around the city.

That's the world I was in, the music and art I was into, and I was big into a lot of these bands. I'd buy their records. I'd listen to the lyrics. But then, when they'd come out for these shows, it was just next-level. They reached for a little extra something, and the shows became about the little extra something, more than they were about the music.

It was all about the *wow.*

One of the biggest wows came from the French DJ SebastiAn, who came out of the Ed Banger Records camp. The Ed Banger label had such an enormous influence on my career—can't stress this enough. More than any other community of artists, the Ed Banger crew helped me rediscover my punk spirit. They were the ones who found a way to inject punk into electronic music, and to fill that space with raw primal energy. We were at the dawn of a new era in electro music, 2004–2005 or so, and it was exciting as hell—almost like there was this brand-new culture emerging from the broader electronic music scene. It was like a complete rebellion—not just in the music but in the attitude. There was something vehemently punk about some of these electro artists, something elegantly and extravagantly hardcore, and I was drawn to that.

Pedro Winter—aka Busy P—was the genius behind the Ed Banger label, the leader of the tribe. He managed Daft Punk when they shot to fame, and we ended up forging a real alliance. Justice would probably turn out to be the anchor of that subculture. Hands down, they were the heart of that movement for me, the gods of the world I was so thrilled to be a part of, but there were influencers all around: DJ Mehdi, rest in peace, a French hip-hop and house producer . . . So Me, who more than anyone else helped to create the look, the vibe, the feel for that moment in time . . . Uffie, who amped up the movement with her alternative dance and synthpop vocals . . .

I felt so aligned with this group, so excited by the energy and the collaborative spirit we seemed to share, that I started to think of them as my French family. I went back and forth to Paris a bunch of times during this period, performed with this Ed Banger collective as much as I could. Out of that, Uffie and I developed such a strong bond we tattooed each other's initials on our arms.

For the first time, I'd come across an ecosystem of artists where I thought I could coexist. Around these guys and the culture they were creating, I was comfortable in my own skin, at long last.

One show at the Moulin Rouge stands out in memory. Think about that for a second: the Moulin Rouge, in Paris's 18th arrondissement, a historic venue that has been around for over a century. Oh, man . . . that night was epic. DJ Mehdi was on the bill. Uffie was on the bill. I was on the bill. We all played our sets and gathered to watch SebastiAn, who opened with an audio sample pulled from the press conference of a French politician who'd been forced to admit to some monumental fuck-up. SebastiAn played the sample on a loop for ten minutes before he played a note of music, and the people in the crowd were gripped, stunned. I thought it was cool as hell.

Here was this guy known for his distorted, disruptive beats—

beautiful, *angry* music in the Ed Banger style—and we were all held by the shame of this disgraced politician, just kind of waiting for SebastiAn to drop some insane beat beneath this guy's confession. I went up to SebastiAn after the show and told him how blown away I'd been by his performance, told him he was truly punk, truly a performance artist. "You just don't give a fuck," I said—my version of high praise at the time. "You do what you do for yourself, and you do it for the moment."

SebastiAn said something self-effacing, sounded almost like he was embarrassed by the compliment, and then he said something about how it was his duty and the duty of all artists to shine a light on these corrupt motherfuckers.

You have to find a way to embrace that, right? You have to want to set people on edge and challenge their expectations and keep reaching for something new. You have to call people out on their shit.

This Moulin Rouge show was a watershed moment for me as an artist, because SebastiAn was putting it out there that there was room in the electronic space for art and angst. I came away from his set feeling like I had a purpose. I wasn't an artist just yet, but with SebastiAn and that Ed Banger crew lighting a path for me, I was starting to become one.

They gave me permission.

This was the backdrop to what I was trying to build with Dim Mak, with our Pickle Patch shows, with my own music . . . and, eventually, with my work as a DJ. Remember, this wasn't exactly the path I'd set out on. The road kind of rose to meet me, and it took me a while to walk it with purpose. It had been a slow build, since college, but it didn't start to happen for me in a big-time way until 2005–2006. Really, it was a long-ass time before I had my own style. I was proficient, but there was no reason for people to remember my sets. I got people moving, was all. I gave them a good time. But after it was done, it was done. Wasn't like I had any kind of following. Yeah, I was doing shows in Los Angeles, doing our own Dim Mak shows, but these were safe, forgiving spaces. I could play my music to a crowd that wanted to hear that stuff, people who maybe knew me a little bit, and I didn't really have to worry about fitting myself into another scene. But then I started getting these gigs in Vegas, where people didn't really know my name or my music, and I couldn't go into my hard electro or indie electro mixes in the same way. At each show, there'd only be a few fans who were really there for what I was putting out, so I had to learn how to be a DJ who plays to the crowd.

The reason I was able to grow from that was because of all these other artists who influenced me, gave me permission to be myself, to break barriers. The Daft Punk *Alive* tour in 2007 was another moment of clarity for me. These guys were the tip of the spear. Busy P was a straight-up maestro when it came to presentation—he injected Daft Punk with this mysterious performance aspect to what they were doing that really challenged people's expectations.

I'd scored my first invitation to Coachella in 2007—although, just being honest, I don't think I was ready for that kind of stage, for such a mammoth festival. This isn't me being humble or self-effacing. No, the moment was a little more than I could handle. In fact, when I took the gig, I was supposed to play on one of the baby stages, on the fringes of the festival. I'd play to folks as they were filing in, but I'd get my performer's ID bracelet, and it was a way to dip my toe in the water, you know. But then someone dropped out of the DJ lineup and they asked me to move into the Sahara Tent, a much bigger stage, so the moment kind of snuck up on me.

I'll cop to it: I wasn't any kind of showman . . . *yet*. I was just a basic DJ, working with my Serato vinyl, didn't have any kind of structure to my sets. Still, it was pretty fucking cool to be invited to the party. (You *always* want to be invited to the party, right?) I wasn't playing at the best time, wasn't on the biggest stage, and they only paid me $1,000 for my appearance, but I was in the mix.

Wouldn't say I'd arrived, but I was getting there.

When I saw Daft Punk at Coachella, I was floored. Yeah, I'd been "promoted" to the Sahara Tent, but I was an ant compared to these guys. It was exhilarating. Every single neurotransmitter in my system was on alert, and it's not because I deluded myself into thinking I somehow belonged on the same bill with these guys. No fucking way. But to see Guy-Manuel de Homem-Christo and Thomas Bangalter light up that crowd and push the limits on what people expected ... it moved me to tears. I was swept up in this beautiful symphony of rage and joy, and when I was set back down in the real world I could only hope to get close to what these guys were doing, in terms of energy and presentation.

Amazingly, the spirit of collaboration was alive and well in the electronic space, so I was able to build on that first Coachella appearance, even if I might have been in a little over my head. In the year that followed, I got the chance to DJ with Busy P a couple times at some of the parties we used to throw in Los Angeles. He'd show up with some of his Ed Banger artists, and I'd fill the room with our Dim Mak artists, and we set out to create this vibrant template for what this type of music could be.

Our lineups were sick: DJ Mehdi, Kavinsky, Thomas Bangalter (without his mask!), Justice, MSTRKRFT, Boys Noize ... It was unreal, what we were able to do together—and yet there was still some ground we needed to cover.

Jump ahead to Justice's 2008 set at Coachella—with me just a plain-old member of the audience after my "debut" the previous year. Everything got ratcheted up to a whole other level. Daft Punk might have lit something in me the first time I saw them perform, but Justice set that something on fire. They played in front of a wall of Marshall half stacks. That's something you didn't typically see in an electronic group. That's rock 'n' roll. That's *literally* a wall of noise, and when Justice dropped their first song the place went nuts. It was abrasive, furious ... unlike anything else. My emotions were on absolute fleek, and the takeaway for me was that our music could be presented in this disruptive way—and here I'd finally started to think of electronic music as *ours* ... as *mine*. Because of all that angry energy coming out of the Ed Banger crew, I was able to connect the music to the hardcore scene that had been a part of me since ... well, forever. It felt more like a punk show than an electronic set, with the way people were stage-diving and circle-pitting and screaming their fucking heads off.

Before Justice, people didn't move all that much at an electronic show. Maybe they'd bob their heads up and down in time to the music, or shuffle their feet a little bit, but here there was unbridled passion, aggression, energy. These guys grabbed the audience by the throat and whipped the crowd into a frenzy. They demanded to be heard. They planted a flag, left us in the middle of a whole new phenomenon.

And I stepped away from that stage thinking for the first time that I could be myself, and tap my hardcore roots, and make the kind of music I was meant to be making all along.

I began to develop more and more of an identity as a DJ, more and more of a following. I was layering in all these screaming, raging hardcore elements to my sets, something nobody was doing at the time. And, playing a lot of my own music—stuff I was recording on my own label with artists like The Bloody Beetroots. Our shows were rowdy and raging. I started stage-diving. Off balconies, scaffolding, whatever perch I could find to make a serious splash. People seemed to really dig it. I was drinking in those days, so that became a part of the performance, too. I'd spray the crowd with champagne—something I still do to this day. It was like this huge, cathartic release, but it also created a great visual, the champagne flying all over, catching the light in these crazy ways. It lubricated the party, you know—literally, figuratively, whatever. Most DJs stood behind a table, or stayed locked in their booth, but I was out there, interacting with the crowd, filling in the spaces between songs with some noise of my own.

Things ramped up after my first Coachella appearance in 2007. I released my first single in 2008—a collaboration with will.i.am, performing as Zuper Blahq. We called it "I'm in the House," and it put me on the map. The lyric was basic, but it spoke to what it was like to be counted in, to be *in the house*:

Don't be blinkin', don't be sleepin'
I be, I be all mine . . .

We followed that up with a Bloody Beetroots collab called "Warp" that became a true electro anthem. We actually released two versions of that one—"Warp 1.9" and "Warp 7.7." Bob Rifo, the Beetroots' leader, and I set it up that way to give a shout-out to the year we were born, 1977. We had no idea the cuts would be so big, but you never really know how people will respond to a song or a remix. I've worked on cuts that felt to me like surefire hits that barely made a ripple, and then I've worked on these small, unassuming side pieces meant to reach a fringe audience that somehow break through. That's kind of what happened with "Warp." It had a bangin' hook, and a simple re-frain that people really responded to, but at the same time it was edgy as hell, loud as hell, powerful as hell. Mostly, it had an intense punk vibe to it, with the kind of abrasive screaming nobody had really put on an electronic record before. I thought it would be cool to attach these rock and punk concepts to this type of music.

If I thought about the public response to "Warp" at all, I would have guessed that some people would dig it and some people would reject it. Like I said, it wasn't designed to be any kind of hit. Shit, it wasn't designed at all . . . it just *was*. If anything, it was meant to push the conversation. At its core, "Warp" was a way to experiment, to put something out there that was like a collision of these two worlds, these two very different types of music.

Looking back, I think one of the things our fans responded to was the defiant message of the song:

I just want, I just want
I just want, I just want
I just want, I just want
I just want, I just want . . .

You know, it's funny (and telling) that when you set out to make a hit record you're almost always wide of the mark. You can't engineer genuine—people will see right through that shit. You can only *be* gen-uine. When you set out to sing your truth, to honor your instincts as an artist, to stand against people who want to tell you what you *can* do in a certain type of song or what you *can't* do . . . well, then you have a shot, and here it ended up that we created a timeless anthem that somehow spoke to an entire generation. To a lot of fans, "Warp" was one of those songs that defined their childhoods, and I'm enormously proud to have had a hand in that, even if we had no fucking idea that it would blow up in this way.

You just never know, right?

Those next couple years, they passed in a blur. People started hearing my name, *remembering* my name, and identifying me with the punk energy and spirit pulsing through the music. Happily, I made enough noise that I got invited back to Coachella in 2009, and this time I knew I needed to step up my game. They were paying me $4,000, and I decided to put that money to work for me. As a DJ, I would put the same thought, design, and structure to my set that bands did. I'd have a set design, a set list . . . a *plan* for how things would go.

I'd been inspired by the killer set designs of my French friends on the Ed Banger label. Daft Punk in particular was doing some big things with staging at this time, with the great pyramid piece they were featuring. And MSTRKRFT, on our own Dim Mak label, was playing in front of an elaborate, eye-popping set. The *presentation* was becoming key, and I started to think I should layer in some stage design of my own. I'd never thought along these lines before, but my thinking was—hey, if the people go nuts for these outrageous sets for the artists they love, maybe they'll go nuts when it's just about the music they love.

My first attempt at stage design, for Coachella 2009, didn't exactly come off as planned. I'd come up with this idea to feature these giant wooden light boxes, with my last name carved out on the side, LED lights flashing from within. It was primitive, but I thought it would look killer, and I reached out to the same guys who did the MSTRKRFT set to build it for me. Ended up costing $5,000, more than I had in my

$4,000 appearance-fee budget, but I dug into my pocket for the rest. Told myself the way the light would pop through those letters—A-O-K-I—would be so totally worth it. Only the way it worked out, it was so totally not, because we forgot to account for the fact that I'd be performing at one o'clock in the afternoon. The effect was completely washed out—you couldn't even see the lights blinking from ten feet away.

Fuck, I was disappointed. It's like I'd taken all that money and set it on fire. But I wasn't too, too down. Instead of playing first, to open the day, I was playing second. Instead of earning $1,000, I was getting $4,000. Instead of playing to, say, 25 percent of a capacity crowd, I was playing to 50 percent. Wasn't exactly big-time, but things were happening. Things were breaking.

Let me tell how that set played out: I hit the stage in an insane Jeremy Scott jacket, bright yellow, that reflected everything. Would've looked *sick* under the glare of all those stage lights I'd been stupidly expecting, but it was still pretty dope under that one o'clock midday sun. Also, I'd brought along a bunch of my hipster female friends to strut and shimmy on the boxes, dressed out in capes we had made from fabrics we found at a vintage clothing store—a striking mix of pinks and yellows and greens and blues.

I had everything worked out, going in—only things didn't *work out* as my set got underway. Some of the "scripted" elements I'd planned on went over great with the crowd, and some fell flat. It was a trial-and-error thing, and it came from a genuine place of me wanting to get people excited, create a little bit of a spectacle, wrapped inside the giant spectacle of Coachella.

First song, I came at the crowd hard—a real banger, to get people moving. *So far, so good.*

Second song, I took off my jacket. *Even better.*

Third song, I shook a bottle of champagne and started spraying it over the crowd. *Everything was firing!*

Fourth or fifth song, I reached for one of the Super Soakers I'd brought along as props. Remember Super Soakers? They'd shoot out this heavy-duty stream, like a water assault rifle—big fun when you're hanging with your friends by the pool or at the beach, but not so much, apparently, when you're in one of the front rows at Coachella, not expecting to be hosed in the face with such intense pressure. In the back rows, people seemed to dig it, but I was pissing off the people in the front row, so I moved off the script I'd written in my head and made a note to myself before reaching for the next element of my show: *Probably should retire the Super Soakers, Steve.*

By the sixth or seventh song, I had my crew bring out four inflatable rafts we'd purchased ahead of the festival. We blew them up backstage, made sure they were nice and full. The idea was we'd put our hipster dancers in three of the rafts, and they could kind of surf-sail across the sea of fans in the front rows. Then I'd stage-dive into the other raft and do my own thing. It was the first time I'd ever done anything like this, but my thinking was—hey, this is a big stage, a big moment, might as well go big.

I'd set it up so we sent the rafts out when I went into my remix of a hot new NASA song featuring Kanye West. The song was called "Gifted," and it was getting pretty popular. . . . I was a huge Kanye fan—in fact, we'd just connected and started talking about finding a project to work on together. I thought the spectacle of those rafts flitting-floating across the crowd fit perfectly with the spirit of the song—and apparently some of the photographers assigned to shoot the festival thought so, too, because there's some great footage of that moment. One of those shots was picked up by *Rolling Stone*, which ran a picture of me in my crazy outfit paddling across a sea of flailing arms in a Coachella photo spread. The editors ran only eight pictures from the festival in that issue, and there's little Steve Aoki, paddling his ass off, alongside giants like Paul McCartney and Radiohead.

Pretty fucking cool, huh?

After a while, I started to think of the songs I played in my shows like acts in a play. It was a level of showmanship that hadn't really been done before—not by a DJ, anyway. I would get out there and sing some of my own shit. I'd stage-dive. I'd bring on some dancers. I'd float my inflatable boat, spray my champagne, reach into my ever-deeper bag of tricks and find some new way to *wow* the crowd—because, let's face it, end of the day, it's the *wow* they remember.

The raft became the centerpiece of my shows. I added it to whatever I was already doing, like jumping off balconies, and that became my thing. I'd find the highest spot in whatever venue I was playing and climb my ass up there and let the crowd know I was about to dive, and then I'd hurl myself onto the raft and people would just lose their shit. Sometimes we'd have two or three or four rafts floating through the crowd, depending on the size of the venue, and fans would climb up into them. They loved it! And I loved it, too. I got this mega-adrenaline rush, every time.

This might have been a shift on the electronic music scene, but it was natural to my history. It was in my nature. I'd been stage-diving since I was a kid, at hundreds and hundreds of shows, so I knew what I was doing. It was in my bones. And here the thing with the rafts just got bigger and bigger. Over hundreds and hundreds of shows, it became a thing . . . a *talked-about* thing.

I was always thinking of ways to add more excitement to my shows. The push was to come up with something unique, an *Aoki* element that no one else was doing. Yeah, I was doing the champagne thing . . . but everyone was doing the champagne thing. Yeah, I was stage-diving . . . but everyone was stage-diving. That was something I borrowed from these great grunge rock artists like Pearl Jam and Nirvana, and now other DJs were stage-diving and crowd-surfing, too—that was getting a little played out, and now it was starting to feel like the raft thing was getting a little played, too, so I started looking at all these other ways I might entertain the crowd.

Around this time, Dim Mak was promoting a Toronto-based duo called Autoerotique. We'd just made a video for their single "Turn Up the Volume," which for some reason featured a bunch of cakes exploding in people's faces as they blew out the candles. In slow motion. The video just kind of blew up, right along with those cakes—people really responded to it. There was something about the powerful incongruity of exploding a cake, something we normally associate with feelings of happiness, that was weirdly appealing, and I carried the images of those cake-battered faces for a long time after we made that video. The tug-and-pull between disaster and celebration. I'd always been into the combustion of two things that don't really go together—the yin and yang of life, you know. And here it got me thinking how I might attach that tug-and-pull to my show, maybe find some way to get the crowd going and then try to shake or shock them.

After a while, I got it in my head to bring a cake to one of my shows. Had no idea just then what I would actually *do* with the cake, but it felt important for me to have one. I was doing a gig up in Boston, so I went to one of the supermarkets in town—I think it was a Stop & Shop. They had a bakery section, so I pointed to a basic-looking birthday cake, put in an order, got them to decorate it with the words "Turn Up the Volume Autoerotique," and that was that.

When I started in on my set, I still had no idea how the cake would play. The way I remember it, it was a raucous crowd. The place was lit. And somewhere in the middle of my set, I dropped that Autoerotique song and reached for the cake. The song was way popular, the video was way popular, so people were into it. They were moving. But they couldn't figure out what the hell I was doing, prowling and prancing up on stage, holding this cake. It was like an incongruous thing—it just did not compute, you know.

Meanwhile, the place was poppin', and I still had no idea what I was gonna do with this cake. As I walked around, people were dipping their fingers into it, stealing a taste, so a part of me was thinking that was how it would go—people would just kind of grab a fistful of cake and get in on the party. But there was this one guy in the front row, a total headbanger, who really seemed to want me to mush the cake in his face. His friends really wanted me to mush the cake in his face. We were all just kind of egging one another on—don't know that anyone thought I would actually do it. I mean, that's a Three Stooges move, right? That's slapstick. That's vaudeville, pie-in-the-face–type shit. Wasn't what I was going for, going in, but the crowd just started cheering for it to happen:

"Cake him!"

"Cake him!"

"Cake him!"

To cake . . . I'd never heard it used as a verb, but here it was. Here *we* were. And it just kinda happened. I held the cake in front of the headbanger's face and he kind of leaned into it and next thing I knew he and his friends were going completely fucking nuts, eating the left-behind pieces of cake, smearing it all over, just having a wild-ass time.

It was like a page out of that great Maurice Sendak picture book we all read as kids, *Where the Wild Things Are*: "Let the wild rumpus start!"

Well, it up and started. Better fucking believe it. And it was wild.

One of the things I learned early on was that when something works you should probably keep at it. It's Branding 101—hit on a successful formula, and then go looking for ways to put it to work to produce the same successful outcome. For whatever reason, this cake thing worked. People dug it—got to be like a badge of honor for the people coming to my shows, to get caked in the face. A rite of passage. They'd leave all that goo and icing smeared all over their faces, leave the cake chunks in their hair and on their clothes, and wear the whole mess with pride the whole rest of the night because they wanted everyone to see they'd been caked. It was like the ultimate souvenir from one of my shows—and, thanks to Facebook and Snapchat and Instagram, they could post pictures and let the world know where they'd been and what they'd been up to.

Eventually, those early 12-inch, 14-inch, 16-inch round cakes grew into the giant sheet cakes I throw into the crowd today, because I found you could cover more ground with all that extra cake real estate, make more of an impact. Eventually, too, I retired the Autoerotique song, because my thing has always been to keep my shows fresh, to find a way to stay ahead of the trends. But the cakes stayed because the cakes *were* the trend. After those first couple shows, people started expecting them. Word spread on social media. Within just a few weeks, fans were coming to my shows with signs saying, "Cake me!" They'd push their way to the front rows, to make sure they were in range— and if they couldn't get hit directly, it was almost as cool to get some cake shrapnel in your face or in your hair—because, hey, second-hand cake looks just as sick on Snapchat as a direct hit.

One sidenote about those first cakes: it just worked out that I grabbed a vanilla cake at the supermarket that day in Boston, and had it decorated with vanilla icing and red lettering. It just worked out the next couple cakes were also vanilla. But then, a week or so in, I had a chocolate cake made—you know, just to mix things up. We were in Seattle, and there was this girl down in front, on some guy's shoulders, just begging for me to hit her in the face with the cake. She had a sign done up and everything. So I caked her, and it was awesome. She was so fucking excited—laughing, screaming, raising the roof with her friends.

Afterward, I brought her up on stage and gave her a towel so she could clean herself off, and when we went into the wings while the next song played she caught a glimpse of herself in a mirror and started crying—like, sobbing.

She said, "It looks like I'm covered in shit!"

She was right. It did. And that was the last chocolate cake I ever threw.

As the whole cake thing took off, I caught some criticism for it. Actually, I caught a shit-ton of criticism. Other DJs called me out as a sellout or poseur, said I cared more about stunts than the music. Soon, some key promoters started piling on, said throwing cakes in people's faces was gimmicky, a cheap gag. They said it was juvenile, stupid, corny. And on some level I could see their point: it was all of that, but it was also so much more. It was a point of connection between me and my fans—a weirdly intimate connection that drew us together, like a group hug. It was this beautiful collision of all these elements that had absolutely nothing to do with each other, and when you put two things together that don't normally fit, people really respond to it.

Mostly, it was a visual, visceral reminder of the joyful abandon at the heart of my shows, at the heart of the music.

Something to celebrate, yes?

The criticism grew to where some prominent promoters wouldn't book me if I insisted on throwing the cakes. Some of them put it to me straight: no cakes, or no shows. Others were a little less clear: they simply didn't book me. So what did I do? I caved, at first. Not because I was afraid to lose out on those big stages, but because I started to think maybe the naysayers were right. Maybe it *was* a little childish for me to be throwing cake in people's faces. Maybe it *did* take away some of the integrity we wanted to see associated with the music we loved, the movement we all helped to create. Plus, when you go to one of those big festivals, you're not just going to see *me*. You're going to see a whole lineup of artists, so I could see how maybe someone who wasn't a fan of mine might not be too, too thrilled to be hit by a mess of cake and icing.

And so I made this big announcement, said I was retiring the cake—changed my whole game plan. And guess what? A lot of those promoters *still* wouldn't book me. It's like I'd stepped in shit, and now it was stuck to my shoe, so they steered clear.

Things have changed now. I'm cool with most of my fellow DJs. I'm cool with most of the promoters and festival organizers. As I write this, we're rebuilding some of the relationships that were a little bit broken over these cakes, but the great lesson here for me was to never make a decision based on someone else.

It's a lesson that applies across the board—no matter what you do, or the size of the stage you happen to be doing it on. You have to trust your gut and trust yourself, even if the outcome isn't the most favorable at first. You have to do what *feels* right. And what feels right, right now, is for me to keep doing what I'm doing. Nothing lasts forever, right? But for now, the cakes are an integral part of my shows. They've become the signature element I was looking for, back when I was starting out.

Been *caking* now for eight years—these days, ten cakes a show, two hundred and fifty shows a year. First couple years, I only threw one or two cakes each night, but there's been a general progression, and when I do the math it comes out to about 15,000 cakes, give or take a couple slices.

(Think that might have something to do with the torn rotator cuff in my left shoulder? My orthopedist does!)

Here's the thing: when I was in the middle of all that cake-noise, it felt to me like I had to make my case, to justify what I was doing to the haters who thought my reliance on props and stunts and special effects was in some way distracting from the music. I set my thoughts down on paper, and the editors at the *Daily Beast* were kind enough to run what I wrote on their website, under the heading "To Cake or Not to Cake"—not exactly a question for the ages, but it kept me up nights, I'll say that.

"These tools of expression are meant to create and amplify energy," I wrote of the bells and whistles I'd started to rely on in my sets. "It doesn't necessarily have to be a cake. Doesn't necessarily have to be a raft. It can be anything that entertains and amplifies that happiness and energy. And in the end, my goal as a DJ is to make people feel something significant, something that they will remember."

That's the endgame here—to leave some kind of mark, make some kind of impression, give the fans who come to one of my shows something to remember. Give them a good time, yeah, but help them to make a memory as well.

DROP

That time I threw out the first pitch at Dodger Stadium? It gets a spot here because it bumps the everyday ways I'd longed to be accepted as a kid into the magical ways I've been embraced as an artist and performer.

Also, it's pretty fucking cool.

It is April 2015. The Southern California sun is shining. The soft, sweet blue of the late afternoon sky sets off the distinctive Dodger blue of my cap—of the caps all around. I play a mini-set on the Dodger dugout before the opening pitch ceremony, to a half-empty stadium. Just a couple songs, using the stadium sound system. People are into it. A lot of the players, they're into it. (Some of them can move, man!) It's not something you expect to see or hear when you head out to the ballpark, and I'm digging that aspect, reminds me of those pop-up, surprise-type sets we used to play back in high school.

I can probably count on one hand the number of times I've been to Dodger Stadium to see a ball game, but when you live in Newport Beach, when you buy into the SoCal vibe and try to move around like you belong, the Dodgers are a big part of that. They're in the air and all around. It's baseball—America's game, apple pie, hot dogs . . . all of that. I've always been big into sports, but as I got older I started paying attention to mixed martial arts, skateboarding, extreme sports where the athletes were pushing themselves beyond human boundaries. Doing all this crazy, wild shit—that's more my thing. But underneath all of that, there is baseball, football, basketball . . . those traditional team sports that bring people together, knit one generation to the next, connect us to our childhoods.

So, yeah . . . the Dodgers, man. The fucking Dodgers. When I get the call inviting me to throw out the first pitch, I think my head will explode. Like, really. This is huge, unexpected . . . cool.

It's an actual color, Dodger blue. There it is, listed in a database of colors, putting it out there that it's a knowable, touchable, replicable thing, and I stand on that pitcher's mound and close my eyes to the moment. People say it's the loneliest spot in all of team sports, the pitcher's mound, and I get what they mean by that. You're standing out there, raised a couple feet higher than every-one else on the field. It falls to you to set the game in motion, to dictate what happens next. All eyes are on you.

The DJ booth is like that, I think. The loneliest spot in the fucking club, only it's on you to whip the room into a fantastic frenzy, to put yourself out there in a way that lets you connect, collide, combust with all that energy.

And so beneath the bill of my cap I am shaded by the blue of loneliness, the blue of expectations, set against the blue of hope and possibility. I think of all the great Dodger legends who wore the team color with pride, with distinction. I think of those who stood on this very mound. Sandy Koufax. Don Drysdale. Fernando Valenzuela. I know enough of the game to know these names, to know what they mean.

I breathe the air they once breathed, kick the dirt they once kicked . . .

Someone thinks to hand me a cake—because, hey, that's how I'm known. If you don't know my music, if you live outside the reach of EDM or hardcore, maybe you know a little of my story, maybe you know my father's story, maybe you know about the cakes. It's the kind of thing, it seeps through the subculture and into the mainstream. And yet this isn't one of those great sheet cakes I typically throw. No, it's just a basic cupcake, tiny, topped with icing to make it look like a baseball, and I'm asked to stand on the mound and toss it to the catcher. It's a little corny, yeah—but, hey, this is baseball. Our national pastime. Wouldn't work if it wasn't a little hokey, a little corny.

There are cameras all over. I go into my windup . . . and the cupcake falls short of the plate. I don't even reach the catcher! I'm humiliated, a little bit. Disappointed, a little bit. Was hoping the thing would thwop and splatter against the catcher's mitt, make a big ol' mess—same way the cakes explode against the faces of my fans. But it just kinda lies there, a couple crumbs splattered in the dirt in front of the batter's box.

Oh, well . . .

Next, I take an actual ball and go into my windup. I have rehearsed this motion in front of a mirror—not a lot, but some. I have taken a couple practice throws—not a lot, but some. I want to look the part. I used to play some, as a kid, so I figure it'll be no big deal. But it is. A very big deal. There are all those cameras. There are all those eyes on me. There is all that history.

And . . . so . . . I choke.

I short-hop the plate on this toss, too. I am humiliated, disappointed again—not a lot, but some.

The catcher runs out to congratulate me and hand me the ball. There is polite applause. The announcer says something hokey and corny over the PA, and I am walked off the field and returned to my regular life.

Jump ahead to where I am now, three years later, pen in hand, setting these thoughts to paper, and I am still struck by the rich, deep blue of the Los Angeles Dodgers.

You can't move around LA without seeing ball caps here and there. Shit, you can't move around the country without running into Dodger fans. I've been halfway around the world, performing in out-of-the-way places, and come across fans in Dodger gear—in Japan, lately, where the Dodgers are known for all the Asian players who wear the uniform. Each time I do, I'm taken back to this moment on the mound at Dodger Stadium. A moment that has come to signal my arrival. A moment that stands now as a reminder of how much work I still have to do if I mean to make my mark.

11

EVERYTHING THAT SHINE AIN'T ALWAYS GONNA BE GOLD

I live my life in collaboration.

The music I make, the artists I produce, the songs I remix and reimagine . . . it's a collective effort.

I cannot create in a vacuum. I can only create in concert with others. We come together in partnership, hoping to find something new in the work, and when we're with each other there's no telling where we'll go, which direction we'll take. We're like those extra balls you put into play on one of those old-school pinball machines—you know, when you collect enough points or hit the right targets in the right sequence and the game gives you a second ball, or a third, and for a quick-burst moment you've got multiple balls careening off the bumpers every which way. Yeah, it's like that. . . . a little bit. We bounce around for a while as one, inside the same moment, until at last the moment passes and the balls drain and our turbo-turn is over.

Best way to share what I do and how I do it is to shine a light on the Dim Mak parties we used to throw in Los Angeles. It wasn't until 2003 that I kicked things into gear at the label and started hiring a bunch of people. Before that, Dim Mak was a loose, one-man operation. I'd go from artist to artist, handshake to handshake, putting out all these different bands I loved and wanted to promote. Sometimes these artists would pop and move on to a major label, a huge career. Sometimes they'd hit and stick with me. And sometimes they'd hardly make a ripple and disappear from the scene, maybe to resurface a couple months later with a new name, a new lineup, a new sound.

It got to where I was dropping a new release every month, and even after I'd been at it a couple years I was still doing it in the same homespun way. I'd hear about a new band and I'd check them out. If I was excited by what I was hearing, if I thought I could make some noise with it, I moved on it. Wasn't about the money for me so much as putting something out into the world that could maybe light a spark, push someone forward, make good things happen for good people.

Those first couple years at Dim Mak, the packaging was all done by hand, on the cheap, on the fly . . . indie all the way. I continued to feature all those little personal touches I'd layered in with my first few releases, like the Hearts and Minds quotes I'd design onto the sleeves, the colored vinyl, the attention to detail. That became our little stamp. Along the way, I learned a couple things about distribution and scale, but other than that, it's like I was still figuring shit out as I went along.

One of the first things I figured out was that there was a tremendous benefit in showcasing new talent, same way we used to do it at the Pickle Patch and Dashain House, so I started staging these Dim Mak events, thinking this was a good way to put a lot of artists in the same room at the same time. This wasn't a calculation so much as a revelation. I didn't have any kind of master strategy or recipe for success. I was simply doing what I'd always done.

Remember, you can't *engineer* genuine. You can only *be* genuine.

Our Dim Mak Tuesdays parties were simply an extension of the Fucking Awesome parties we used to throw, and the Pickle Patch shows we used to stage in Santa Barbara, only now we weren't playing to a bunch of kids. We were playing to people in the music business, people with something to say, people with the juice to make things happen. Just like when I was back in college, there was this tremendous sense of community sprouting up around Dim Mak, this feeling that we were all in on the ground floor of something special. We were all about the new talent, and jump-starting careers, but now we were also all about making connections, and putting together like-minded souls looking to change the culture and grow their music in new ways.

At bottom, I was the same kid who collected all that vinyl, idolized all these bands, soaked in the hardcore spirit . . . but at the same time I guess I was evolving. I was on the constant lookout for something different, new . . . *special*. And when I thought I'd found it, I'd try to prop it up so others could see what I was seeing, hear what I was hearing.

It was in this heady environment that I first met Kanye West—in 2006. In the history of Dim Mak Records, these were still early days for us, but we'd already had a lot of big-time successes. It was almost to the point where just having the Dim Mak seal of approval was enough to put an up-and-coming artist on the radar—like a self-fulfilling prophecy, you know. And each time one of our artists hit, the rep of our little label got a little bit bigger.

Then as now, Kanye was digging into the underground scene, same as me. He was a fixture in the clubs, always had his ear to the ground, listening for the next big thing. He came to one of our parties one Tuesday and we got to talking. I remember posting a picture of the two of us on Myspace (that's how long ago this was!), and out of that one night we formed the beginnings of a working friendship. We talked from time to time. We traded ideas. It was usually Kanye initiating these exchanges, because he was moving on a much higher plane and I didn't want to crowd him or come across like I had my hand out, but I was always happy to hear from him—it was an honor, really. A year went by, and then another. I could go months without hearing from him, but then I'd hear from him a couple times a night and we'd be like those two runaway pinballs, bouncing in all these different directions. He would flit in and out of my life in these random ways, always with a ton of enthusiasm for whatever it was that had him reaching out to me in the first place.

That was Kanye: he was all over you, all about you . . . and then he'd move on to something or someone else.

Sometime after we first got together, Kanye had this tour he was mounting with Lady Gaga, and he asked me to help him create a bunch of interstitial-type music—connecting beats or hooks that might serve as bridges between songs. He seemed to want his show to be all of a piece, all the music linked in this seamless way, and he wanted me to help him create this music. I was psyched to throw down on this, but I never really had a clear idea what he was looking for, and we never really went into the studio, but we kept talking about it and talking about it.

And then, just like that, he moved on.

That's just how it goes when you're working with a mercurial genius. Kanye's mind seemed to run a million miles a minute. I hadn't heard from him for a stretch, but then one night I was on tour in England, and my phone started buzzing. I was in the car with my manager. I noticed Kanye's name on the readout and I was like, "Holy shit! It's Kanye West."

I could hear in his voice that he was super-excited. He wanted me to check out these bars he was working on—couldn't spit them out fast enough.

Now, I'd been making music for fifteen years by this point, and no one had ever called to ask me to listen to their rap—so the simple *fact* that he'd reached out like this was enough to get me going. Still, to this day, no one else has ever called me out of the blue to get my take. So, yeah, I was blown away a little bit. Thrown a little bit. I mean, this was Kanye West—a big, big deal. So I put him on speaker, told him I had my manager with me in the car.

And Kanye just went into it, told me to check out his flow.

It was a weird, wild moment, to be driving through England while this mad poet-genius-rapper sat in his studio half a world away, spitting these new bars by me . . . and wanting to hear what I thought. But Kanye was like that, I was getting. He had this ever-changing collective of five or six people in his orbit, people he wanted to work with, people who maybe inspired him in some way, and for this brief period, if you were one of those people, you'd hear from him all the time. Until he moved on to the next group of people who led him off in some new direction.

Anyway, he killed it. You could almost feel the energy-charge in his words, crackling through the speaker on my cell phone—one of those magical kick-ass moments you just know will stay with you forever. I knew this in my bones, as it was going down. But then, before I could really say anything, he had to hop off the call, and we never really followed up on this—the song he was working on, it just kind of hung there between us, unfinished, bouncing through the sound waves over the blue of the Atlantic Ocean and evaporating in the atmosphere.

Next time I heard from Kanye was after I did my remix of that NASA song I wrote about earlier. (Another shout-out to my friend Sam Spiegel, same dude who'd lent me his turntables for my first paying gig—he started NASA and asked me to remix this song they had out that just happened to feature Kanye.) Remember, that song—"Gifted"—was blowing up in the clubs, but outside of the EDM world, it wasn't getting a whole lot of play. I was struck by the frenzy of that song, loved Kanye's verses, so that's why I decided to play my remix at Coachella, and it must've been a good call, because that was the collision of music and moment that caught that *Rolling Stone* photographer's attention.

Kanye's lyric on that one was dope:

I'm known for runnin' my mouth
I will not be accountable for what comes out, uh . . .
I dunno, I might have said it
I was kinda gone and light-headed . . .

I sent the remix over to Kanye, and he flipped for it. He reached out after Coachella and said something like, "Holy shit, man. That's so sick. And what's with the motherfucking raft?"

Soon as we reconnected over this Coachella moment, I was back in Kanye's orbit again, and we started talking more and more about making some music together. It was all very vague—but then, before we got going, he changed his whole musical direction. He basically reinvented himself—something he's done a bunch of times throughout his career. And somewhere in that reinvention, whatever we were supposed to be working on together was lost.

Okay, so that's the first beat to the Kanye riff I want to share. I'll come back to him in a bit, but for now I want to splinter off and tell the Drake piece to the same story, because the one bleeds into the other. Here's the Drake riff: it was the summer of 2009 and we were both walking in the SLS Hotel parking lot one night in Beverly Hills, chasing the same parties. He noticed me before I noticed him. He was with his crew. As I was walking, I heard, "Aoki?" I was texting on my Black-Berry (that's how long ago *this* was!), so I didn't think anything of it at first, but then I heard it again: "Aoki?" I turned, and there he was, with his manager Oliver El-Khatib and the rest of his crew. He said, "Yo, it's Drake."

I couldn't fucking believe it, couldn't believe I'd made Drake say my name twice before turning to see who it was, before he figured he should probably introduce himself. I mean, these were early days for Drake, but he was already a big deal. Everybody wanted to fuck with Drake. He was probably one of the most talked-about artists on the scene, at the front end of a white-hot moment that's still burning for him, all these years later.

We'd never met, but of course I was psyched to see Drake, told him what a big fan I was, all of that. He had his crew with him, and we all stood around talking. We kicked around the idea of maybe finding something to work on together, and the talk seemed more genuine than the usual Mutual Admiration Society–type bullshit you some-times hear in these encounters. And then, when it came time to part, Oliver took me aside and told me all about OVO—Drake's record la-bel, October's Very Own—and filled me in on what was going down with Drake, what was coming up. He took my contact info, and told me about this song Drake was about to drop called "Forever"—said, "Maybe you could do a remix."

I said, "Alright, sweet! I'll do any song with Drake. Just tell me when."

Well, *when* turned out to be pretty damn soon, because Drake's team sent over the stems that week. My jaw dropped when I opened the files. That song blew up pretty much the moment it dropped—and when Drake spit the opening lines of his rap they seeped straight into the culture: "Last name Ever, first name Greatest . . ."

It was iconic!

The big surprise here, for me, was that Oliver hadn't said anything about who was on that cut with Drake. Turned out "Forever" featured raps from Kanye West, Lil' Wayne, and my favorite rapper of all time, Eminem. Holy shit! That just made the track triply iconic. Somehow, Drake had put together a lineup that was like the Dream Team! Mount Rushmore! It was the biggest remix package I'd ever opened, hands down, and I was in complete fucking heaven.

And then, when I opened Kanye's a cappella track, I just about shit. He was spitting the same bars he'd shared over the phone with me on that transatlantic call. I played those bars and thought, *I know those lyrics!*

Check it:

Big fame, big chains
I stuck my dick inside this life until that bitch came
I went hard all fall like the ball teams
Just so I can make it rain all spring

That shit is *hard*, man. You don't forget lines like these, even if you're hearing them through a cell phone, on the fly. And now here I was, hearing them in this whole new context. I was struck by the way the world comes full circle, with the way all these different artists kept coming into my life. Like those crazy pinballs, set loose all at once. It got me thinking how a lot of us keep circling the same material, the same ideas. This deal with Kanye was just the example at hand, but it was a killer example: here was a lyric he'd been working on some years earlier coming back to me now with a completely different intention. But that's how all true artists work, right? There's no such thing as a bad idea—only an idea that isn't fully formed, fully realized. The great ones find a way of holding on to these little half-formed snippets of art and truth and moment and finding a way to slot them in when the time is right, when the thought is finished.

Some songs, they're like a fine wine, or a bourbon that still needs to age. Sip from that glass too soon, and you won't taste the full effect.

Best to let it sit until the right moment—to let it breathe . . . until all these moving parts come together in just the right way.

Now, you're probably wondering how that "Forever" remix turned out, and I wish I could say it was a ridiculous success, but it wasn't like that. In fact, just being honest, it was probably one of the most mediocre remixes I've ever done. It was workmanlike, efficient . . . but that was about it. I played it for a while in my sets, because when you have this fresh cut featuring all these superstar artists, that's what you do, but I wasn't really feeling it. My fans weren't really feeling it.

I don't even listen to it anymore, that's how mediocre I thought this track was—but that's how the process works for me. It never even had an official release. It ended up that we gave it away for free on my blog, but I didn't think it was strong enough to see the light of day in a full-on way. That's how it goes sometimes—and my thing is, I try not to beat myself up about it. I tell myself, Hey, some shit works, and some shit doesn't. The idea is to maybe learn a little something from your hits *and* your misses. Me, I'm constantly learning new things, trying new things, working to become a better producer, remixing so many different tracks. You take what comes your way, you take what you can from it, put your little stamp on it, and then you move on to the next one.

By this point, I'd remixed thirty, forty songs. A lot of them we never put out, and it all goes back to what I wrote earlier, about how you never know how things will play. All you can do is grab at the opportunities that come your way and try to grow from each one. If people come to what you're doing, that's great. (That's the whole fucking point!) If they don't, you try to learn from it and move on.

Each time out, I put it to the fire. Then I wait to see what happens.

That's kind of where my head was at when I met Kid Cudi. How that came about was I was doing a tour with my friend Atrak, who had his own label, Fool's Gold. We put together a Dim Mak/Fool's Gold US tour that happened to feature this hot new rapper he'd just signed who was out with his first single, "Day 'n' Nite." That was Scott Mescudi—Cudi!—and he was an electric talent. You could see straightaway that this kid had something special. Flosstradamus was with us on that tour, with a bunch of other acts, and we played all over the country in small concert halls and clubs, and it was one of the first tours I was on since I'd made it as a DJ where it felt like I was in a band again. We all hung out together, stayed onstage for each other's sets, got to know each other. A lot of good, tight friendships came out of that tour, and Kid Cudi and I had this great bond.

After the tour was over, he called me to tell me about a track he'd just laid down with MGMT and Ratatat, which he said had this cool indie vibe to it. He said it had his signature sound, but at the same time it was way different from anything he'd done.

He said, "Can you remix this for me?"

I said, "Are you fucking kidding? Of course."

This was before I'd even heard the song. I was already a fan of MGMT and Ratatat, and I would have done anything for Kid Cudi at that point—he was my brother.

So he sent over the stems and I got into it. The song was "Pursuit of Happiness," and it's like it came from another planet.

I'm on the pursuit of happiness and I know
Everything that shine ain't always gonna be gold

In all, I made about sixty different versions of that song. That was unheard of for me. Typically, I'd play around with a song for a while, have some fun with it, then send it off and hope people would like it. But there was something different about this cut. It got under my skin, into my head. I built it up to where I was feeling all this pressure, so I kept going at it. The song was so otherworldly, I wanted to find a way to connect it to all these different crowds. There was this small electronic scene that I was representing, alongside the indie scene we had going at Dim Mak, up against the rapper-from-another-planet vibe that Cudi was bringing, and I was determined to connect all the dots.

I kept hacking away at it, and Cudi threw in with me and got into it as well—helping me to switch things up with the drum sounds, for example, when I was looking for the slightest shift in the kick. It took me a couple months to get it right, I blew right past my deadlines, but I told myself I really needed to nail this one.

Thing is, after all of that, I went back to my second or third version and decided I had it right from the start. The simplest line was where I needed to be. So I grabbed some elements from my later versions and mashed 'em all up into what eventually became my "Pursuit of Happiness" remix. What I liked about it was how it featured a strong sense of the rave element in the song, how Cudi's spacey hip-hop sound came across, how MGMT and Ratatat's indie influence really popped. It all came together in a way that left you wanting to really rock your face off to the song.

We dropped that remix and I had the highest expectations. We all did, I think. But, end of the day, it faded away. We made a little bit of noise with it but not much, and not for long. It was a bit of a sleeper, that cut—it came and went, and I started to think of it as a fail. It went into the "miss" column for me, and I was disappointed. Surprised, too, because I really thought this one would take off, but mostly disappointed.

But then in 2012 this movie came out called *Project X*, and the remix was featured in a prominent way, so the song had a new lease on life. And it wasn't just a song they played over the credits, or in the background underneath some throwaway scene. No, it was highlighted in this climactic moment in the story, and echoed the whole point of the film, and when the movie took off the remix took off right along with it. People around the world started listening to my remix on the back of that movie, and a couple years after that the song got a *third* lease on life when DJs like Hardwell, David Guetta, Martin Garrix, and Tiësto started featuring it at peak times in their sets, all over the world. I offer this story here to show how these hits can sometimes sneak up on you. Or maybe they ultimately do happen in the ways you imagine, but it takes a while for them to get there. Some songs are like the one or two duds you find in that box of firecrackers you set off on the Fourth of July. At first they might just fizzle, and you're waiting and waiting for them to pop and nothing much happens, but then you look away for a beat and they start exploding.

This was like that . . . a little bit.

And this was also a reminder that when you collaborate with all these brilliant artists, when this abundance of talent comes together in a kind of harmonic convergence, you tend to forget that you're also collaborating with the universe. Sometimes the timing isn't right, or the stars are not aligned in the right way.

Sometimes you need to fizzle for a while until it's your time to pop.

A lot of people forget that I was a performer, a promoter, a producer, a record label "executive" . . . all *before* I was a DJ. For a couple minutes, I was even a manager.

Here's that story . . .

Very quickly, Dim Mak Records had become my vehicle to promote new bands. It was an extension of who I was as an artist, an outgrowth of the music I'd wanted to make as a kid, laying down those first tracks on my TASCAM recorder. Like I wrote earlier, it took me a while to give up the ghost on my career as a musician—all those bands I'd been a part of, playing to all those tiny crowds . . . I finally took the hint. And now here I was with Dim Mak, going to shows, looking for the next breakthrough artists, trying to put my own little spin on the scene.

I wasn't alone in this. There were a lot of folks trying to spotlight new talent. The editors of *Fader* magazine were among the best at identifying artists who were about to pop. They'd put people on the cover before anyone knew who they were, and just a couple months later they'd be everywhere. They were exceptionally consistent in this—way, way ahead of the curve, and almost always on point. More than any other publication, *Fader* sat at the crosshairs of hip-hop and indie rock culture. They understood what was happening, could see the trends as they were taking shape. When they said something or someone was cutting-edge . . . well, then it was so. Knox Robinson, then *Fader's* editor in chief, was actually one of the first to spark to what we were doing at Dim Mak, and to shine a light our way, and out of that we developed a good relationship. They supported me, so I supported them—by making our artists available at their parties and events, by playing for them at South by Southwest when I started to DJ . . . whatever.

Knox called me up one day to tell me about this Sri Lankan singer his magazine had just put on the cover. She was out with a new song and Knox thought it would be big, big, big. He was right, as always. I watched the video and I was fucking floored. The artist, of course, was M.I.A., and the song was "Galang," and it was dazzling. I'd never heard anything quite like it—a mash-up of dancehall, jungle, electronic, and world music. You could tell that M.I.A. had a certain "it" factor about her, an impossible-to-define *something*, a chance to become the next big pop artist in America. I loved her voice, her sound, her style . . . over time, I'd come to admire her activism as well. I was super-excited and wanted to find a way to support what M.I.A. was doing. After all, that's why I'd started Dim Mak in the first place—to promote all these different artists, from all these different cultures, representing all these different types of music and ways of thinking. Like a melting pot, you know.

Just to be clear, it's not like I came away from watching M.I.A.'s "Galang" video with all these dollar signs in my eyes, dreaming of what she could become on the back of that one single. Wasn't like that. Yeah, money was a part of my thinking, but only a small part. The real fuel for me was giving a leg up to emerging artists who maybe needed a boost. The money was important only because it takes money to make the right kind of noise. And because money coming in would seed the process, and put me in a position to do the same thing all over again, for the next artist who came along who could use a push.

Knox mentioned that M.I.A. didn't have a label in America, was only signed to XL Recordings (one of my favorite labels, based in the UK). His thought was that she was definitely looking for an indie label to feature her in the United States as well, and since Dim Mak was pretty well known as a purveyor of breaking talent, he thought we'd be a perfect fit. So he kindly put me in touch. Dim Mak was an easy sell—at least, to M.I.A. We'd already had some success with artists like The Kills and Bloc Party, taking these English bands and introducing them in the States and helping them to build an audience and some momentum, so I was able to make a good case for Dim Mak. We didn't have the infrastructure back then to put out anything more than a single, but that would be enough to get M.I.A. some traction, and to help her move into something bigger. I understood that progression.

M.I.A. and I got to talking. She was down to work with us, but then when we started moving forward we got some pushback from her "small" label in England. It turned out they had the rights to her song tied up worldwide, and there was no room for an indie label like Dim Mak in her deal. That was cool. I mean, I was disappointed, but that's just business, right? Still, I was like a dog with a bone. I wanted to find some way to work with M.I.A., because I thought she was uniquely talented. I loved what she was putting out there, wanted to see things happen for her, wanted to have a hand in *making* some of those things happen for her, so I suggested she take me on as a manager. It was a big, ballsy ask, but I figured I didn't have anything to lose, so I just put it out there. M.I.A. was down for this arrangement as well—a big, ballsy move on her part—so I went to work. I met with every major label, every major record executive: Capitol, Universal, Atlantic . . . the same folks I'd been hitting up for Bloc Party. I teamed with a hustling A&R pro on this effort—a woman named Riko Sakurai, who used to work for Def Jam—and together we covered the waterfront, hoping to make things happen for M.I.A. in the States. Dim Mak was a known entity by this point. We had a bit of a rep, so I was able to trade on that to get these meetings, while Riko called on some big-time connections of her own, and M.I.A.'s obvious talent did the rest.

Our thing was to sell M.I.A. as the next Madonna—that was the hook. She was international. And so for a couple weeks I was running around Los Angeles, taking all these meetings, and the whole time M.I.A.'s UK label was giving her more and more pushback. They wanted to know who this Asian kid was in the States making all this noise on their artist's behalf. They had it in their heads that they would be handling her worldwide, and they were pissed that this nobody with an upstart indie label was going around blowing all this smoke about someone they thought was *their* artist.

These guys fucking hated me. *Hate* is a strong word, but here it applies—they *hated* me, thought I was irrelevant, an irritant, something to get past. Mostly, it was M.I.A.'s UK manager who hated me, thought I was just some punk. Who knows, maybe they were right to call me out on this, but M.I.A. had my back. She loved that I was so passionate about her music, about her career. She loved the hustle I brought to the table. So she stood up to her manager, for a while. Until she couldn't. In the end, the suits kept me from continuing on in this role, but for a couple months I think I helped get M.I.A. out there and noticed and talked about in the industry. It laid the groundwork for the reception she'd find in the States. Of course, she's so enormously talented she would have no doubt popped on her own, without my rookie efforts, but I like to think I helped her along, even just a little.

The great takeaway for me out of this one brief experience I had as a manager was that when you're passionate about someone or something, it can bring you to great places. But in the end, passion can only take you so far. It might be enough to get you the gig, but it won't let you *keep* the gig. For that you need a whole bunch of shit to fall your way. You need a team of people around you who believe in you and what you're putting out there. You need experience.

You need folks working *with* you instead of *against* you.

Basically, you need to play to your strengths, instead of to the best-case scenarios you have in your head. It took me a while, but I figured it out. Just look to the hip-hop album I released in 2017—*Kolony*, featuring young artists on the verge of cultural explosion. That was always my thing, trying to spotlight talent a couple beats before an act broke in a big-time way, so here I lined up a bunch of artists who were about to take off on this massive career trajectory—like Lil Uzi Vert, Lil Yachty, Rich the Kid, Migos. There was also room under this tent for collaborations with established hip-hop stars or veterans in the field—like Ma$e, Gucci Mane, T-Pain, and 2 Chainz . . .

Before *Kolony*, an entire album of EDM-infused hip-hop was unheard-of. Yeah, artists from both worlds have gotten together on songs, onstage, but not on this kind of scale. As concept albums go, this one was pretty high-concept, but as soon as we got the idea for it we were running with it, hard. Wasn't a hard sell to get these artists to work with me on this—I'd worked with a lot of them already, so it was just a matter of creating the right material and coordinating our schedules. The key to making a project like this work is the excitement that happens in the combustion of these two different worlds, but that's the kind of thing that gets me going. When I team up with other artists, it's like I slip into an extra gear. I'm like a kid again, a fan. I try to find a way to make the music matter most of all, and the business side of what we do falls away. My creative juices start to flow. And this is especially so when I tap artists who work in entirely *other* genres— like the song I wrote for a 2015 collaboration I did with Linkin Park, "Darker Than Blood."

Darker than the blood
Higher than the sun
This is not the end
You are not the only one

That was definitely a career highlight—for the chance it gave me to work with a band I grew up listening to. From *Hybrid Theory* on, Linkin Park was essential listening, the soundtrack to a ton of key moments in my life. For years, whenever an interviewer would ask me if there was one singer I wanted to work with, I'd say Chester Bennington—so when it finally happened I was over the fucking moon. And now, with Chester gone, I look back on the music we made together and I'm so, so grateful we had a chance to collaborate on something so, so meaningful. I just kept putting it out into the universe until it finally happened. It was beyond a dream come true, and when we were in the studio together I took a moment to step back from what was going on and consider the career I'd managed to build from my life-long passion for music . . . *all* kinds of music. The ways I've managed to work with so many different artists, from so many different genres. We share the stage, we share our audiences, we drop these songs to-gether and give each other the room we need to do our thing—separately, together, whatever . . .

Pretty fucking cool, huh? And, way more effective than trying to shoehorn my way in as a manager.

One of the other shape-shifting lessons that found me as I began to collaborate with artists is that there is a wellspring of power to be found in the ways we take care of each other and lift each other up on the back of our efforts. When I was coming up as a producer and DJ, it was so incredibly validating and humbling to me when next-level art-ists like Kanye West and Drake reached out and said they wanted to work with me, and I think the young artists I was trying to promote or advance at Dim Mak, like M.I.A., felt the same way when I reached out and said I wanted to work with them.

Underneath all of that, there's often another element at play that makes these collisions of talent so rewarding . . . and it finds us in the form of basic human kindness. What do I mean by that? Well, it's probably best to *show* rather than *tell*, so I'll share the story of the time I connected with the outrageously talented producer Brian Burton, better known as Danger Mouse, who burst on the scene with his pioneering mash-up of Jay-Z's *The Black Album* and some instrumentals from the Beatles' White Album. Slam those two classic albums together and what do you get? Danger Mouse's *The Grey Album*, an experimental piece Brian put out in 2004 that became one of the most talked-about albums of the year. What a lot of folks forget about that album was that it was a bootleg. In a lot of ways, Danger Mouse made a name for himself on the back of this album but never put it out in any kind of official way. He didn't have any of the licensing in place, but he was still able to make some serious noise with it—that's the DJ culture, on full display.

Really, I can't overstate the impact that one album had, all over the world. It was exciting as hell . . . especially to *me*. See, I was still finding my way as a DJ, and I'd been stoked by all these genre-bending mashups that were coming out around that time. They weren't remixes, exactly. They were something else . . . something *new*. There were these Belgian brothers I was following back then called 2 Many DJ's, and they'd mix Beyoncé with Nirvana and Dolly Parton—clever, genrebending, time-hopping stuff. They were elevating DJing and mash-ups to a whole new level in an incredibly witty way . . . totally fresh. I just loved it, tried to incorporate some of that technique into my sets, so when Brian came out with his first bootleg version of *The Grey Album* I reached out to him, to see if we could connect on a project.

Brian knew the Dim Mak brand, knew what we stood for. We were breaking a lot of young artists in those days, especially in Los Angeles. We had a ton of cool indie bands in our lineup that were just blowing up, so we were on people's radar. At the time, Brian was putting out music on a bunch of different experimental hip-hop labels, like Warp Records. I was trying to think of some way to release his music on Dim Mak, but he was already signed to this legendary label, so I got the idea to team him with an indie band I was really into at the time called Sparklehorse, led by a guy named Mark Linkous. Mark was making very eccentric, very spacey music that seemed to fit with the fusion-type music Brian was focusing on. If Sparklehorse was into the idea, we could get them with Brian and they could perform together as Danger Horse.

(The other option would have been to call this side project Sparkle Mouse, but Danger Horse seemed so much darker, more mysterious.)

Turned out Brian loved Sparklehorse, so he was down, and once Mark Linkous and them were on board I told them I wanted to do it as a Dim Mak release. In my head, I worked it out that since Danger Mouse was already signed to another label and Sparklehorse was signed to Capitol Records, this mini-super-grouping would be Dim Mak's way in.

Turned out, too, that there were a shit-ton of hoops we had to jump through to get both artists cleared to work on this project, but somewhere in all that hoop-jumping Dim Mak was squeezed out of the deal. The Capitol execs were all over this idea, but they didn't want Dim Mak involved. They essentially said, "Look, Sparklehorse is our artist. They're not signed to you. And Danger Mouse isn't signed to you, either, so you don't belong in this project."

But that's how it goes sometimes, right? You set all these wheels in motion, and they end up rolling away from you. In big-picture terms, thinking globally, I was pumped that this one idea would actually grow into something, even though I was bummed, thinking locally, that there was no room in the project for Dim Mak. I didn't even get a production credit out of the deal, but I told myself that was cool, too, because these artists I loved got to work together in this compelling new way.

Of course, that was the public spin I put on the deal. Privately, I was pissed. The entire project had been my idea, and even though I'd come up in the music business in a kind of DIY way, even though my early efforts had been all about seeding and feeding the community and not turning everything into a money-grab, this one left me a little steamed. It told me that despite whatever success I'd been having, whatever success I *thought* I'd been having, I still didn't have the power to make things happen on my own. I was still just the little guy, and the little guy always gets stepped on, right?

The Danger Horse album didn't do a whole lot of business, didn't get a whole lot of publicity, but a lot of people came to believe that

Brian's work on the album elevated him to a whole new level as a producer. The collaboration allowed him a platform to show what he could do in the studio, and out of that he became one of the top producers in the music industry. Understand, that transformation-elevation didn't happen overnight, but it happened over time. Just look at the artists Brian has produced over the years, in addition to his own side projects as Danger Doom (with rapper MF Doom), Gnarls Barkley (with CeeLo Green), and Broken Bells (with the Shins' frontman, James Mercer): the Black Keys, the Red Hot Chili Peppers, Norah Jones, Gorillaz, U2, Portugal. The Man, and on and on. Dude went on to earn nineteen Grammy nominations, including a sick total of five nominations as Producer of the Year. (Oh, and by the way, out of those nineteen nominations, he's walked home with six Grammys, including a 2011 Producer of the Year nod—huge!)

Okay, so that's all in the way of setup for the story I *really* want to tell about Brian Burton. We'd stayed in touch in the couple years since we tried to get together on that Danger Horse project. I followed what was going on with him, he followed what was going on with me, and it was all good. And then it just worked out that we were getting on the same plane, headed to London. We ran into each other in the airport. I was flying to one of my first big shows as a DJ—things were really starting to happen for me, so I was excited to fill Brian in. And he was eager to tell me what was going on with him in the studio, what he was listening to, who he was working with, all of that. Trouble was, I was headed to the back of the plane, in one of the last rows in coach, while Brian was seated in business class—that's kind of where we were in our careers. But Brian seemed to want to keep the conversation going, was maybe looking for someone to keep him company on the long flight, so he told me he'd stow his gear and his guitar in business class and work his way back to me at some point.

Next thing I knew, before takeoff, he was offering his seat to the guy next to me and sitting down in his spot so we could keep talking—only we didn't talk all that much, once we took off. It was more about hanging out than catching up. Still, he stayed there the entire flight, and it struck me as one of the sweetest, warmest, most genuine gestures I'd ever seen from an artist of his stature. To give up his business-class seat to hang with me, in a shitty-ass seat in one of the back, back rows, practically in steerage . . . that kind of thing just isn't done.

Think of it: Brian's guitar flew to London business class; the complete stranger who was meant to be sitting next to me in coach flew to London business class; and Brian sat his ass down at the back of the plane. And like I said, it's not like we talked the entire time. I drifted off to sleep at one point. He drifted off to sleep at one point. And whenever I'd startle myself awake and catch my bearings, I'd look over to Brian and think, *What the fuck is he still doing here?* The whole thing was just so remarkable, so outside my experience . . . so validating and humbling.

It's the little things, right? The small, sweet gestures that remind you we're all just trying to connect with each other on a basic human level. That's where kindness kicks in. Decency. Generosity. The good turns we find it in our hearts to drop on each other, they stay with you. This totally surprising, totally unnecessary gesture from Brian Burton, it stayed with me. Same way it stayed with me that time Kanye West started rapping to me over the phone, just to get my take. Same way it struck me how M.I.A. didn't really know me or all that much about me, and yet she liked the energy and enthusiasm I was putting out so she decided she wanted to work with me.

Where's the *blue* in these stories, in this message? I've got no fucking idea. Maybe it has to do with the water we need to help all the seeds we plant in our lives and careers to flower into something meaningful, purposeful. Yeah, let's go with that. Let's go with the idea that when we sprinkle all these prospects all over the damn place, when we nurture all these different relationships, it sometimes works out that they just don't work out. Or that we'll never get to see if they grow into what we've imagined, never know if other people might happen by and start to water or fertilize or tend the area where we were working and take it on themselves to grow the thing into something *they've* imagined, like the world is some community garden. But when we do get to see what we've sown, we can step back and smile and think, *Just look! Behold this beautiful thing!*

No, I cannot create in a vacuum. I can only create in concert with others . . . and sometimes this is how those concerts happen.

DROP

Shit is going down.

Hard.

I don't know this at this moment. Not yet. For now, I am blissfully, stupidly unaware. I am dead asleep.

It is Sunday, October 1, 2017. I have spent the day at the hockey game, of all places. The Golden Knights, our new team in town. The T-Mobile Arena was lit! Was just an exhibition game, didn't really count, except it felt to me like all of Vegas was there. There was a group of us, "The 75"—they brought us out, had us up to the owner's box. We'd gotten together on this, lent our names, our voices, to the push to bring an NHL franchise to town, and now here we were, rooting for our new home team like they'd been here the whole damn time. And so in this one way, at least, the game counted. It counted because it counted us in.

We were big league. Welcome to Vegas, baby.

It was a late-afternoon game, and I remember feeling kind of tired after. All that energy, all that whooping it up, it can suck the juice right out of you. Anyway, I was dragging. The plan was to meet up with some friends after the game. Middle of the game, we were texting, figuring when to meet up, whether we'd head over to this country music festival at the butt end of the Strip.

The festival, it wasn't a typical outing for me, but I was down. I listen to anything, everything. If it moves me, it moves me. If it's got heart . . . if it comes from a place that's right and true . . . that's all I need to hear. Genuine is genuine, right? Country was so not a part of my culture growing up. But I learned to sing along. I was fascinated by the stories inside the songs. The heartbreak. The melancholy. The hard-charging work ethic. Out of all that, I was even inspired to do a collaboration with Lady Antebellum, one of the top country groups around, out of Nashville.

Anyway, this show tonight, the Route 91 Harvest Festival, it was big. People flying in from all over. A lot of my friends would be there. But when I set myself on the couch after I returned home from the game, I nodded off. Can't be sure, but I think I was still wearing my Golden Knights jersey—the swag they gave me when I got to the game. Don't know what it was had me feeling so tired. Guess my body clock was off. Or maybe I just wasn't meant to be at the festival, that's all. Whatever it was, I was out.

Oh, man . . . I was gone. Like I said, dead asleep. Out to where nothing could touch me. Nothing at all.

But then it finds me, through the fog of dreams, through the life I have made, the playhouse I have built, the stories I tell myself to shield me from the world around.

A friend's voice startles me awake. Something about a shooter on the Strip. Something about the sheer fucking craziness of it all.

Something . . .

The words don't stitch together in any kind of consequential way, not at first. They're just words. But they align in my head soon enough, and when they do I find myself grabbing for more information. Like a toehold . . . a purchase . . . a way to process. I know these bits and pieces, but I want to take in the whole damn thing, all at once. I want to see what I'm hearing, feel it in my bones, swallow it all up, and the way to do this, I tell myself, is to turn on the TV.

So there it is . . . here it is . . . only it takes a while for what I'm seeing to register. I've got all these words lining up for my attention, this bulletin from my friend waking me up to tell me what's going on, these bulletins from these local news reporters on the scene, and now on top of that I've got all these images to absorb as well. It takes a couple beats for everything to coalesce.

WTF?

I mean, if ever there was a moment where I wanted to throw up my hands in desperation, frustration, indignation . . . this was it. Like, seriously, what the fuck? What I was seeing, hearing, made no sense. There was no way to attach it to anything in my experience.

Just no way.

We tend to forget what these terrifying moments are like when we're in the middle of them, when they unfold for us and become clear. Maybe it's because of the chain reaction they set off, the dominoes they start to topple. Maybe it's because what we're seeing, hearing, is so outside our experience there's no room for it in our thinking.

It takes a while for us to adjust our sets, you know.

By the time you read these words, months and months will have passed. You will know all about the holes this asshole gunman fired into our lives, but when I zap on the TV, nobody knows shit. I don't know shit, and yet I am awash with feeling. If there is a color to my moods, then I am every color in the rainbow, every color in the cosmos, every color in music, every color in nature. There is red, white, and blue . . . mostly blue. There is anger, confusion, terror, sadness. Above all, at just this moment, there is worry.

What is the color of worry? I actually put this question

out into the universe, as if I expect to find that what I am feeling can somehow be seen. As if there might be a science to it. An essence. As if all these words and images can line up in a way that begins to make sense, and morph into a fine film. A prism. A lens. Through which I might see these moments as I see myself. And as this last notion crystallizes, and lingers, it all becomes clear. I am flattened by the thought that I could have been there at this country music festival, should have been there, by thoughts of the people I know who are probably there, right this fucking instant, desperately seeking cover, just across the desert from my playhouse in the hills.

I am rocked.

I reach without thinking for the phone on the table in front of me. I find my friend Dan Bilzerian's phone number. There is no answer, so I try again. Nothing. But I know he's there, we were supposed to meet up, so I check on his Snapchat story and see that he is running through this scene of complete madness, mayhem. It's like a bulletin from the front: frantic, chaotic video, underneath the sounds of frenzy and chaos. I can make out the sounds of gunshots beneath the blur of images. I can hear Dan's voice: "I just saw some girl's head blown off."

I am fucking stunned.

I am blue, with sadness.

I am black, with grief.

I am black-and-blue, a deep fucking purple, a bruise that might never heal.

The rest of the night passes like a nightmare. It is eleven thirty. It is midnight. It is tomorrow morning.

I stand with my friends on my deck overlooking the Strip, the lights from the Mandalay Bay Resort, from the Luxor, from the festival, filling the sky with false hope. There is every color in the rainbow, and a whole bunch more you won't even find in nature—the neon juice of my hometown, lit in a way I no longer recognize. The city seems close enough to touch and a million miles away, all at once.

Our world is on tilt.

We hold each other close, and cry, and imagine that we are stronger together, that we can somehow lift ourselves from this dark, uncertain moment simply by standing next to each other. We fumble with our phones, trying to get through to the friends we know are on the scene. There is still no word from Dan, only the trace evidence we find on Snapchat—sounds and images that don't leave any of us feeling reassured that our people are okay.

We're getting news updates on our phones. All these horror stories lining up for our attention, each of them told from a deeply personal place. And the weird thing is, as we take it all in and try to process it, we're looking out across the desert at this picture-postcard view, and the Strip smiles back at us, same as always. There is no mood to the Vegas skyline, seen from a distance. There is only skyline. Our whole world has been shot to pieces—but then, when we look up, it's all so right there, looking pretty much like our world, still whole.

It takes a while, but a storyline emerges. A picture becomes clear. Colors come into focus. Colors we've never seen before, never even considered. We learn that Dan's buddy Dee Jay Silver finished his set just before the shooting began. We learn that Jason Aldean was on stage when the first shots rang out, getting the crowd going with "When She Says Baby," one of his anthem-type songs:

> Some days it's tough just gettin' up
> Throwin' on these boots and makin' that climb

The first reports say there are multiple shooters. Eyewitness accounts tell us shots are being fired from up and down the Strip. Nobody knows the situation—our phones are blowing up with a hundred rumors. The most accurate reports keep finding us on Snapchat, punctuated by the tinny, tiny sounds of automatic gunfire: rat-tat-tat-tat-tat. The sounds are almost cartoonish, ringing beneath jittery images of complete fucking madness. It is difficult to grab at the enormity of what we're seeing, hearing, the tragic weight of it, underneath those rat-tat-tat-tat-tats.

To call it all surreal is to give these dark, desperate moments a poetry they do not deserve.

We're taking turns texting, calling, crying . . . our eyes drawn to the after-hours silhouette of our city. My million-dollar view, shot all to hell. Vegas is on lockdown. People have been shut out of their hotels, turned away from the Strip. Concertgoers are fleeing the scene with nowhere to go. All they know is the need to get away, away, away . . .

Fight or flight, man . . . what it comes down to, in the end.

I put it out there that all are welcome, if they can make it up to where we're at. Friends and friends-of-friends and friends-of-friends-of-friends start to turn up at my front door.

Next thing I know, I'm getting a text from my DJ pal Jauz, who's in town from San Francisco. He's with our friend Tiësto, and another friend, Billy Blatty, and all three of their girlfriends, and they're up against it. They can't get to their rooms—because for a tense couple hours, city officials worry there could be multiple shooters at multiple locations, and the hotels and casinos on the Strip are sealed shut. I tell them to find their way to my place.

Finally, two o'clock, maybe three, I get Dan Bilzerian on his phone. He's back at his house. Thank God. We start out texting and switch to FaceTime. His voice is small, quiet. He's been deep in the middle of some scary-ass shit, but he's not saying much. He tells me of the girl he helped to carry to an ambulance. He tells me how he doubled back to the scene like Rambo, but he does it in this soft-spoken way, like he's shell-shocked.

We talk about our friends who may or may not have been at the concert, friends who may or may not have checked in.

We are taking inventory. There's nothing to do but worry and shuffle around, waiting for clarity.

Eventually, suddenly, I drop back onto the couch that claimed me earlier. It is three o'clock, four. I need to power down, quiet those worst-case scenarios. There's just too much to take in—too, too much.

I close my eyes.

Next thing I know, it's Monday morning. Early. I don't remember sleeping. I don't remember dreaming. One moment I am sitting, shaken, and the next I am slapping myself awake. The sun is just up. There are still a couple friends on my deck, still looking out in disbelief at the horizon—I guess, trying to make sense of the horror and the terror of the night before against the certain backdrop of the Las Vegas Strip. When I was in New York on September 11, 2001, this was a little like that, the way people found a rooftop or a vantage point with a view of downtown, black smoke still filling the sky, trying to somehow process the horrific images they saw on TV alongside the ghostly aftermath scene that's spread out in front of them.

There's a chill in the air that has more to do with what-ever happened last night, whatever's happening still, than it does with the cool of morning.

I am black-and-blue—the color of getting the shit beaten out of you by a world you can't quite know.

From here, we move into triage mode. Last night was about piecing together the puzzle of what was going down, about getting a head count on our friends, about looking inside the madness.

This morning is about doing what we can.

I call a doctor friend to see what's going on. He tells me the local hospitals are low on blood, so I put the word out on social media.

Later, I hear the lines to donate are eight hours deep, so I put it out there that the folks looking to give blood could use some water, some snacks.

My city is broken, and I am flattened, shattered. I am scrambling to do what I can. It feels like nothing but it is everything.

No, I'm not running back into that shitstorm with a gun, like my friend Dan. But this is me, clawing my way back to whole. This is me, trying to make sense of it all.

Somewhere in all of this, a hashtag appears. A movement takes shape. We are #VegasStrong. It rolls and gathers, builds in force. Those of us broken and blue, we find each other online and will each other whole. Soon we are all knitted together in this same-seeming community, bound by our shared outrage, our shock, our grief.

We are joined in mourning, and healing. And hope.

We are blue. All over.

12

UNFUCK THE WORLD

hortly after my father died, I set off on a journey to learn everything I could about the human body. I was in the middle of that downward spiral I wrote about earlier, drinking heavily, trying to find a fucking toehold. In the fog I was in, it made no sense to me that a man so full of life, a man so driven and fiercely determined to live, work, and play at the very highest level, could be cut down when there was so much life left to live.

It killed me that my father wouldn't get to see how *all* the stories of his life would play out . . . wouldn't get to see how his children turned out.

What killed me most of all was the thought that I could have saved him. It was a stupid thought, a baseless thought . . . but there it was. He'd had the best doctors, of course. And what the hell did I know, anyway? But still, I was desperate to learn if there was anything I could have done for him—and, out of that desperation, maybe, to learn the things I should be doing to take better care of myself and the people I loved.

I went off on a kind of information walkabout. I read everything I could find about health and wellness—mainstream stuff, *out there* stuff, everything in between. Books, blog posts, journals . . . I even started watching a bunch of documentaries on mind and body issues—a total-immersion deal. Somewhere in there, a friend recommended a book called *Anticancer*, by David Servan-Schreiber, a cofounder of Doctors Without Borders and a fifteen-year brain cancer survivor. His story was incredible. He'd been given this grave diagnosis, but then he went off in search of all these ways the body itself can fight off cancer. He started eating the right foods, eliminating stress, living a more spiritual, purposeful life, embracing all these transcendental Eastern principles.

I tore right through that book, and the great takeaway for me was that we're wired in such a way that cancer and heart disease and dementia and all these other illnesses can't help but find us in the Western world. Basically, we're screwed. We put all these toxins into our bodies, breathe in so much shit, run ourselves into the ground . . . we give ourselves no chance. But Dr. Servan-Schreiber did such a complete 180 with the way he changed up his lifestyle he was able to beat his cancer. Twice.

Dr. Servan-Schreiber's account left me doubling down on my quest to learn everything I could about the human body. I wasn't thinking globally, just locally. I wanted to share what I was learning with my mother, with my siblings . . . maybe do what I could to keep us in each other's lives for as long as possible. My family at first thought I was a little nutty. I was super-evangelical about it—same way I'd been when I had that come-to-Jesus moment following my one and only acid trip back in high school. (With me, when I get passionate about something, I can sometimes go overboard when I look to share that passion with the people I care about.) But after a while I started thinking outside myself on this, outside my family. The more I learned, the more I realized there were fundamental changes we should *all* be making, on a societal level, that could maybe set right the planet, you know.

One thing I want to make clear: I didn't know shit about nutrition, going into all of this. I'd always been active, but I didn't know shit about fitness. I'd been a vegetarian for a stretch, because of the folks in the co-ops I used to live in back in college, but that was just me fitting myself into the community. That was just me going along. When I left Santa Barbara, I went back to eating like crap—lots of carbs, lots of greasy, starchy processed foods. Maybe I'd pick up on some new diet or trend and try that out for a while, but I had no idea what I was doing, and I never stayed with any of these new diets or trends for very long.

Another thing I want to make clear: this wasn't about community. This was me, looking out for me and mine. This was self-preservation—but, hey, when you're out to save your ass and you keep an open mind, you start to see that what applies to you and yours applies to the many.

Eventually, my reading took me to the books of Ray Kurzweil, the great futurist and inventor. Probably the first book of his I read was *The Singularity Is Near*, which talks about the ways the human body can overcome the destiny of biology. Oh, man . . . the guy is so outrageously brilliant, and even if you spend just a little bit of time with his books he finds a way to distill all of these complex ideas into a simple, fundamental truth: technology can radically extend and enrich our lives.

That one basic thought set me off on my walkabout in a whole new direction.

I reached out to Ray and we struck up a friendship, and in a lot of ways that friendship was the inspiration for my first *Neon Future* album, with an introduction from Ray Kurzweil himself, in which he welcomed listeners to our shared neon future and promised that we would soon see "radical life expansion, not just radical life extension." That album was a breakthrough for me. It featured collaborations with artists like Fall Out Boy, Afrojack, Machine Gun Kelly, and will.i.am. It also gave me one of my first mega-mega-hits—"Delirious (Boneless)," featuring Chris Lake, Tujamo, and Kid Ink, with over 100 million streams . . . and counting!

Can't nobody stop us
We're gone delirious . . .

But mostly *Neon Future* marked the first time I was able to use my platform as an artist to bring about change—*meaningful* change. That's something I'd been passionate about since the early days of Dim

Mak. You could see it in a small way with those Hearts and Minds motivational quotes I included in the liner notes, putting out all these healing, hopeful messages. But I'd never made any kind of major push on the back of my own work, and here I got to thinking that this DJ thing wasn't just about making a name for myself, or making noise with my music . . . now it was *also* about making some kind of difference. End of the day, that's why we're here—to make the world a better place.

Like a lot of artists, I'd set up a charitable foundation to help fund a bunch of projects and initiatives, but we were a little all over the place. When we started out, our mission statement was to crowd-source a portion of the proceeds from each of my shows, letting the fans decide where the money would go. The idea was to promote a kind of "party with a purpose" concept, and to get people talking about the issues of the day, and feeling like they were helping to make an impact—only the crowdsourcing piece didn't really work. Nothing against my fans, but they tended to respond to whatever was going on in the news in that moment. That's just human nature, right? And it's an instinct that came from the right place. If there had been some natural disaster in the news, they'd vote to send the money to relief efforts there, so that's what we did.

Don't get me wrong, I was pleased and proud to be a kind of con-duit in this—pleased and proud of my fans for thinking things through in a thoughtful way. And I was thrilled and grateful that there was enough money coming in that I could send a good chunk of it right back out and put it to good use. We'd vet the organizations and send the money along, and it would make a little bit of a dent in whatever it was that was going on . . . until the next disaster or crisis came along and turned our attention to another corner of the world. But as my interests away from music became more and more centered on health, I decided to ditch the crowdsourcing element and channel all these resources into the science and study of the human brain. That became my primary goal—an obsession, really. I was out to support organ-izations in the brain science and research areas with a focus on regen-erative medicine and brain preservation, but money alone didn't cut it.

A lot of these organizations were already well funded. Where they were lacking was in being well understood. People just didn't *get* the seismic advances that were happening in the field, didn't see that we were on the cusp of fundamental change, so I also started talking about it, posting videos and interviews and links to important new research, hoping to get my fans thinking of a world where degenerative brain diseases do not exist and we're able to tap all these new ways to extend and enrich our lives.

One of the first organizations we donated to was the SENS Research Foundation, a group of scientists and innovators based in Mountain View, California, that believes a world free of age-related disease is possible. It's a beautiful dream, don't you think? But to the forward-thinking folks at SENS, it's not just a dream, it's a reality. SENS stands for Strategies for Engineered Negligible Senescence. "Negligible Senescence" is a term coined by Dr. Caleb Finch, of the University of Southern California, who found that in some animals, the progressive decline into sickness and frailty as it relates to age is negligible. In creatures like lobsters and hydra, it's pretty much non-existent. You can study them in the seabed, and they don't seem to age. Whatever physical abilities they have once they reach maturity, they pretty much keep, with no deterioration over time, which led Dr. Finch and others to conclude that there must be some way to tap into that for us human animals, some way to thwart any and all age-related pathologies.

The SENS Research Foundation is run by a guy named Aubrey de Grey, who wrote a book called *Ending Aging*, in which he really breaks it down. He talks about what it means to age, how cells degenerate, all the different ways they can wreak havoc on the body. You should read his book or tune in to one of his TED Talks. What I love about Dr. de Grey is that he doesn't just *know* his stuff. He knows how to *sell* his stuff—meaning, he can talk about it to just about anyone, in clear, simple terms. I've had him out to the house a couple times, and we sat in my studio and talked about the transformative power of music, the healing powers of meditation, the remarkable resilience of the human brain . . . real next-level stuff. Obviously, he did most of the talking, and I did most of the listening, but the thing that got me most excited about Dr. de Grey's work and the work of his colleagues was the way they were able to share their discoveries and put them out into the world in an accessible way.

You listen to him and you start to think, *Oh, man . . . anything is possible! Everything is possible!*

It's exciting as hell.

One of the other things Dr. de Grey turned me on to was the way the brain responds to color—that's been one of the main themes of these pages, so we might as well end on this note. It's like I said on the very first page: *Sometimes I think my whole life can be seen through shades of blue.* That's not just a line or a literary device or a way in to my story. No, it's the color of my life—the fucking base coat. My name, my moods, my music . . . there's a blue to match 'em all. But it cuts deeper than that. We've known for centuries that certain colors attach to certain personality traits, deep down, but there's a science to what we've known. Colors trigger our neurotransmitters in such a way that they create or enhance mood, based on different amplitudes and wavelengths of light. The color blue has been shown to activate our parasympathetic nervous system—meaning it sends a signal to our brain that there is no danger present. That's where we get our fight-or-flight impulses, and when we're bathed in blue we can shut down that part of our brain, because there's not a whole lot of call for either.

When we're in a blue state, we're good to sit and chill and let our minds roam.

Think about it: when things are calm and peaceful, when there's an overwhelming presence of blue in your environment, it stimulates deeper abstract thinking. When our defenses are down, there's no need to feel agitated or up against it, or to put ourselves on high alert. It allows us to turn our thoughts and our energies inward, in a purely positive way. Shit, maybe that's why artists and poets and visionaries have always been drawn to the sea, where the blue that reflects off the ocean helps to free our minds and ignite our creativity. Don't know about you, but I always feel most alive when I'm on the water, most at one with the world, and I have to think it ties back in some way to the feeling of calm that finds us in a blue state. When we don't have to think about surviving in the moment, we're free to come up with ideas that move us, that move others, that move humanity forward.

We were sitting in my recording studio—the Neon Future Cave!—when Dr. de Grey pointed this out to me, probably because I'd had the room decorated with the sweet electric blue of that first-generation BMW i8 interior I wrote about earlier. That was the car of my dreams when I was a kid, and I was still drawn to it. The color was striking—and I guess it struck something in Dr. de Grey. He explained to me how without really realizing it I'd laid in a foundation to be my best creative self. In that kind of blue-soaked space, he said, I can relax, feel safe, and free my mind to explore. Against that kind of blue backdrop, we can take care of our basic needs: eating, sleeping, breathing, fucking . . .

That's the power of blue, hardwired into our system.

That's the power of blue, woven into the carpet, painted on the walls, dyed into the fabric of the upholstery.

And so I finish these pages the way I started out, talking a blue streak about ways my life has been colored in blue tones. I can't tell you why this is so, only that it is so. I can't fully explain the science behind it, only that there *is* a science behind it. I can't even grasp the poetry of it, as I live my life in the hottest part of the flame, in the shade of the blue tree of my family's history. And I can't tell you what it is that draws me to these various shades of blue, to the blue markers that stamp my soul, only that they keep me whole, and calm, and present, and productive as hell.

I am so fucking thankful that music has taken me to this place—the music I write, the music I remix, the music I listen to. When I started out in this thing, the music was all about finding myself, creating community, seeding our little subcultures with a feeling of belonging, a feeling of purpose. And now it's just worked out that my community has grown. My sense of self has grown. The little subcultures where I lived and breathed, like straight-edge hardcore, they've been put on blast, to where they now fill up the vast spaces of the EDM movement and seep past the edges of hip-hop and punk and good old-fashioned rock 'n' roll. It's viral . . . it's international . . . it's around every damn corner, and I stand proudly in the DJ booth, counting my blessings that I've been gifted this chance to contribute to the soundtrack, you know.

Together, we're making some serious noise, and we'll *keep* making serious noise—*I'll sleep when I'm dead!*—but underneath the movement we've built and the music we're making there's still this pulsing hardcore mandate to make the world a better place. To put in more than you take out. To lift each other up, triumphantly. To set each other down, compassionately. To make repairs. It's embedded in the culture, so that's what I'm trying to do as I look to our shared neon future, and to the pioneering research of organizations like the SENS Research Foundation that seek to understand what it means to be human, after all.

I do not have all the answers, when it comes to the workings of the human brain, or how we might tap technology to help us live longer, more productive lives. Truth is, I don't have *any* answers, but I'm learning what questions to ask. I'm learning that it takes money and a platform to bring about these pioneering breakthroughs—and that these breakthroughs, in a vacuum, will be locked in a kind of theoretical limbo. We need to talk about this shit, understand this shit, embrace this shit . . . so we do what we can to keep the conversation going.

And while we're doing that and figuring it all out, we might as well paint the walls blue.

ACKNOWLEDGMENTS

The writing of a book is very much like the collaborative effort that goes into a song. It takes many hands, many minds, many moods . . . a whole lot of coming together before you can step back and see what you've got. I didn't know this going in, but I know it now, and I am indebted to family, friends, and fans who helped me revisit the stories of my life and set them down here. It's amazing the shit you forget, when you're busy living your best life—and even when things aren't going so great. The power of collective memory is just as amazing.

First and foremost, got to call out my family: my dad, rest in peace; my mom; my siblings—Kevin, Grace, Echo, Devon, Kyle, and Jennifer; my cousin Taku and his wife, Cheryl; my brother-in-law Brent; my nieces and nephews—Olivia, Natalie, Noa, Hunter, Alessandra, Eleanor, and Bella. I love you all, wouldn't be me without you . . . wouldn't have anything to write about, really. So, thank you. Like, a ton.

I am grateful as well to Dan Paisner, who worked with me to synthesize the stories of my life and find my voice as a writer. It's one thing to write a song lyric, you know—a book is a whole other animal, and here I think we tamed the beast.

Sylvan Creekmore, our editor at St. Martin's, also rates a nod here, together with her creative, hard-charging colleagues at St. Martin's Press, including Gabrielle Gantz, Steven Seighman, Young Lim, and Ryan Jenkins, and the copy editor, Janet Byrne.

Thanks to Eve Attermann of William Morris Endeavor who was able to persuade the good people at St. Martin's that I could (and should!) write a book. (This was *before* she persuaded me, by the way.) Thanks as well to my music agents at WME: Joel Zimmerman, Kirk Sommer, Kyle Bandler, and Marc Geiger.

Of course, I couldn't do what I do without the support of Matt and Dougie at Deckstar, who put up with my shit every single day of my life—as well as Andre and LV at Deckstar, and Michael at Seminal Management, who help with the heavy lifting. They take care of business, so I can bounce around the planet making beautiful noise.

At Dim Mak, shout-out to Lee, Bryan, and Lorne; to Brandon at my Dim Mak Collection fashion label; and to Patrick and David from Ultra. Oh, and can't forget my Aoki Foundation and Pizza Aoki teams . . . they are *on* it!

At home and on the road, I'm supported by my personal assistant and trainer Martin, who keeps me fit and fed and (somewhat) organized; by my tour manager Dillon Anderson (can't imagine life on the road without him); and by Mike The Connect, who lives up to his name every day. And, by my talented and tireless road crew: Sam, Caesar, Alex, Crazy Chris, Jim and Mike from Film Tank, and Jay and Cam at Nightride . . . I'm indebted to you all.

To all the futurists and visionaries who have challenged me, inspired me, and helped to shape my thinking—J. J. Abrams, Ray Kurzweil, Bill Nye, Aubrey de Grey, Tom Bilyeu, Jim Qwik, Yuval Harari, Elon Musk, Neil deGrasse Tyson, Bill Bryson, and Daymond John—thanks for lighting a path and stoking my spirit.

To all the artists, producers, songwriters, DJs, and musicians who've lit every kind of fire in me . . . to all the promoters who keep putting me on their stages . . . to all the people who believed in me when they didn't have to . . . and, to all the people who shit on me and made me fight harder to do better . . . thank you, thank you, thank you.

And finally, to my love Nicole, my poofish, who has added all kinds of new colors to my life. I'm so glad you're here on this journey with me—let's keep enjoying the fucking ride.